# MUSIC
## OF THE
# HEART

## John & Charles Wesley
## on Music and Musicians

*AN ANTHOLOGY*

CODE NO. 1592

## Carlton R. Young

Preface by Richard Watson
Foreword by S T Kimbrough, Jr.

**Hope Publishing Company**
CAROL STREAM    IL 60188

Available in the United Kingdom from:
Stainer & Bell Ltd.
P.O. Box 110, Victoria House
23 Gruneisen Road
Finchley, London N3 1DZ
Telephone: 0181-343 3303
Fax: 0181-343 3024

FIRST EDITION

ISBN # 0-916642-58-5
Library of Congress Catalog Card Number 94-073036

# Roger Neil Deschner

## 1927-1991

Friend and colleague whose life was
music of the heart

# CONTENTS

# PREFACE

The music in my heart I bore
Long after it was heard no more.

Wordsworth's lines from "The Solitary Reaper" are a reminder that the simplest ideas, and the clearest expression, are often the best. And it is in this spirit that Carlton Young should be commended for having given his scholarly attention to two primary elements of the Methodist sensibility. The first was the religion of the heart, inherited from the seventeenth-century puritan divines, what Richard Baxter called "heart-work and heaven-work": the Wesley brothers, who knew and treasured their puritan heritage, also loved Herbert's poetry, and would have remembered that "Come, my way, my truth, my life" ends triumphantly "Such a heart, as joys in love." John Wesley found the heart in the German hymns from the Moravian *Gesang-buch*, such as Paul Gerhardt's *O Jesus Christ, mein schönstes Licht*, which he translated so beautifully:

Jesu, Thy boundless love to me
No thought can reach, no tongue declare:
O knit my thankful heart to Thee,
And reign without a rival there:
Thine wholly, Thine alone, I am,
Be Thou alone my constant flame.

He called the hymn "Living by Christ": living, that is, by the heart that had been so "strangely warmed" (what a wonderful word "strangely" is in this context!) and keeping within itself the "active flame" of the Holy Spirit. In Charles Wesley's hymn it becomes the heart-altar:

O Thou who camest from above
The pure celestial fire to impart,
Kindle a flame of sacred love
On the mean altar of my heart!

Carlton Young puts this into the context of John Wesley's sermons, especially the early one based on the astonishingly daring metaphor of "The Circumcision of the Heart": "No man has a title to the praise of God unless his heart is circumcised by humility."

The second element of early Methodism was its music. Dr. Young's pivotal chapter, "Music of the Heart: Lyrical Religion," makes it clear that the key element in the early Methodist tradition was not so much the humility of Wesley's sermon as joy and praise, the turning of theology into "lyrical religion," into a powerful combination of belief and song. Lyrical religion was, in S T Kimbrough Jr.'s words, quoted here, "a 'sung' theology, or at least a theology expressed in poetry and song." It allows the imagination to awake, and the heart to leap for joy.

This awareness prompts Dr. Young's two principal sections, on John Wesley as "Tune Book Editor and Music Critic" and on Charles Wesley as "Lyrical Theologian and Music Critic." It is an appropriate and informative division; and although Dr. Young's "Afterword" modestly says that "my expectation is that this volume will prompt additional research and commentary," it is clear that he has already done a great deal of both in this book. He provides much useful material: the references in John Wesley's letters, and in the journals and diaries, and his work on the *Foundery Collection*, together with his instructions for good congregational singing, are found here. These may, as he suggests, be material for others to work on; but they represent a very substantial contribution to knowledge in their own right.

John Wesley did not like anthems, or what he regarded as affected or ostentatious singing—"a psalm which no one knew, in a tune fit for an opera, wherein three, four, or five persons sang different words at the same time!" Charles was more tolerant, if only because of his friendship with J. F. Lampe, and because his sons were notable musicians in their own right. There is a delightful vignette of a concert by them in Charles's house, with Uncle John present "and, as he confessed, a little out of his element, though he spent an agreeable hour, but preferred plain music and plain company."

John Wesley had the good sense to realise that "plain music," sung by congregations modestly and sensibly, attracted and kept his followers to the paths of duty and righteousness, gladdened their hearts, and refreshed their spirits. And so, in the inspired words of the Preface to the 1933 *Methodist Hymn Book*, "Methodism was born in song." Dr. Young's book reminds us of the truth of that marvellous sentence: so does the hymn which it inspired, Brian Hoare's "Born in song!" (*Hymns and Psalms*, 486), a joyous recreation of that first mood of exaltation and rejoicing in the people called Methodists. Indeed, one of the reasons why this book is so central—and so moving—is that it takes the reader back to an early and pure Methodism, to an eighteenth-century world of misery, despair, and spiritual neglect, in which men and women would embrace poverty, discomfort and condemnation to travel the length and breadth of the country preaching the words of salvation and love to the marginalised and the despairing. In a beautiful passage from *Adam Bede*, George Eliot describes one of them, Dinah Morris, preaching on the green at Hayslope—

> Where a crowd of rough men and weary-hearted women drank in a faith which was a rudimentary culture, which linked their thoughts with the past, lifted their imagination above the sordid details of their own narrow lives, and suffused their souls with the sense of a pitying, loving, infinite Presence, sweet as summer to the houseless needy.

It is this lovely, simple, almost primitive and magical quality of the earliest Methodist years that is the context of Dr. Young's book. "Let us sing a little, dear friends," said Dinah Morris at the end of her sermon; and as the traveller pursues his way, like Wordsworth's passer-by in "The Solitary Reaper," "the voices of the Methodists reached him, rising and falling in that strange blending of exultation and sadness which belongs to the cadence of a hymn." How these things came to be is the subject of Dr. Young's book: I hope it will be read by many Methodists (and others) and that it will delight them, and instruct them, and inspire them.

Richard Watson, Professor of English, University of Durham,
Vice-President, The Charles Wesley Society

# FOREWORD

What distinguishes John and Charles Wesley as eighteenth-century Anglican divines who founded a Methodist movement?—the inner witness of the spirit, faithfulness to the prayers and sacraments of the church, sound preaching of the word, praising God in song, the wedding of personal and social holiness? Yes, but all of these facets of their lives and ministries issue from a religion of the heart. That is their raison d'être. John Wesley expressed this eloquently in a stanza of his translation of a Paul Gerhardt hymn:

> O grant that nothing in my soul
>     may dwell but thy pure love alone!
> And may thy love possess me whole,
>     my joy, my treasure, and my crown.
> Strange flames far from my soul remove,
>     my every act, word, thought, be love.

Charles and John Wesley discovered that the most effective means to create the personal and corporate memory of a heart and life filled with self-emptying love is in music of the heart—a uniting of text and music in a symphony of aesthetic emotion, musical/poetical art, and intellect with Christ's self-giving love at the center. Therefore, they committed their lives to shaping the musical and textual memory of God's people. They formed a lyrical theology by which the faith community could remember who it is and what it is to do. Charles became the lyricist, and John, though also a poet, became the astute collector of tunes.

For the first time scholar, pastor, and student can turn to a volume about the role of music in the life and ministry of the Wesleys, the emerging Methodist movement of the eighteenth century, which includes an absorbing collection of the brothers' own comments about music in prose and poetry. Carlton R. Young has combed the sources and produced a collage of "documents of the Wesleys on music." It is a first-rate source book that brings together in one place what the Wesleys said about the religious, cultural, technical, moral, aesthetic, inspirational, amusing, personal, and corporate aspects of music. The volume is an imperative for understanding the unique contributions of Methodism to religion of the heart or lyrical theology. Church and music historians will find the collection of documents and excerpts invaluable to a careful study of the eighteenth century.

The thorough coverage of John Wesley's collections with some innovative analysis of Wesley's appropriation of texts and tunes moves beyond James T. Lightwood's earlier work at a number of points and is an interesting complement to the section on tunes in volume 7 of the Abingdon Press *Works of John Wesley*. Young covers the broad spectrum of Wesleyan influence from the folk tune "Nancy Dawson" to the astute composers of eighteenth-century London's West End and Covent Garden, George F. Handel and John F. Lampe, who composed music for Wesley texts.

While parts of Young's volume are intended to be a documentary reader without extended commentary, chapters 2, 3, and 6 provide perceptive theological reflection on music of the heart in eighteenth-centu ry England and Methodism and new directions for the future.

This is an interesting companion to St. Augustine's treatise *On Music*, for the Wesleys show the way for Christians to be "an alleluia from head to foot." Young has erected important signposts of direction along this way: the unique contributions of the Wesleys and the Methodist movement to lyrical theology, the first parallel study of the musical contributions and opinions of Charles and John Wesley, excerpts from Charles Wesley's *Journal*, letters, and poetry on music and hymns, a survey of John Wesley's contributions from the *Charlestown Collection* (1737) to *Sacred Harmony* (1780). Here is a valuable source book for the study and interpretation of musical, theological, and historical currents in the eighteenth century, particularly those with which the Wesleys interacted. I hope it will inspire a long-overdue interpretive process of "Music of the Heart."

S T Kimbrough, Jr., President
The Charles Wesley Society and
Executive Secretary of Mission Evangelism
The General Board of Global Ministries
The United Methodist Church

# Introduction

During the eighteenth-century Wesleyan revival John and Charles Wesley produced hymnic repertory, including tune books, that possibly exceeds any previous or subsequent Christian movement. Charles Wesley's output alone is estimated to be about 9,000 sacred poems and hymns. Since most Christian hymnals have continued the use of many of Charles's texts (or hymns), Charles's work has been the subject of more commentary and scholarly research than those of any other English-language hymn writer. The Hymn Society of Great Britain and Ireland through its *Bulletins* and the continuing work of the Wesley Historical Society in its *Proceedings* have been instrumental in the study of his work in the twentieth century. In the USA in 1990, the Charles Wesley Society was founded to coordinate the continuance of these efforts in Great Britain and the USA and elsewhere.

Music, music-making, musicians, and singing are usually acknowledged as important concomitants of the eighteenth-century Wesleyan revival. John Wesley produced three tune books—*Foundery Collection,* 1742, *Sacred Melody*, appended to *Select Hymns with Tunes Annext,* 1761, and *Sacred Harmony*, 1780—and rendered opinions on appropriate music and performance practice for Methodist societies. Until early in this century, however, coverage of the musical contributions of the revival and its leaders, John and Charles Wesley, for the most part was incidental to hymnological study and biography.

The musical contributions of the Wesleyan revival, particularly the three tune collections edited by John Wesley, were first researched and evaluated by James T. Lightwood in "Notes on the Foundery Tune-Book," 1900; "Tune Books of the Eighteenth Century," 1905; and *Methodist Music in the Eighteenth Century*, 1927; and by Maurice Frost in "Harmonia Sacra by Thomas Butts, I and II," 1952-53; "John Wesley's Hymn Tunes," 1944; and "The Tunes Associated with Hymn Singing in the Lifetime of the Wesleys," 1957-58. These trace the work of and comment on John Wesley as music critic, compiler, and editor.

Nelson F. Adams continued the examination of Wesley's influence in his unpublished doctoral thesis "The Musical Sources for John Wesley's Tune-Books: the Genealogy of 148 Tunes," 1974. Adams' research and commentary, though admittedly dependent to some extent upon the formative work of Lightwood and Frost, greatly advances our understanding of John Wesley as music editor, compiler, and publisher of collections that include a wide range of standard English hymn tunes and folk melody, German folk melody and choral tunes, and adaptations of opera and oratorio theater-style music. Adams includes photocopies of each page of the *Foundery Collection*, 1742, *Hymns on the Great Festivals and Other Occasions*, 1746, the 1770 edition of *Sacred Melody*, 1761, and the 1788 edition of *Sacred Harmony*, 1780.

Nicholas Temperley in "Reform Movements, 1760-1830," *The Music of the English Parish Church*, 1979, relates the music of the Wesleyan revival to other developments in evangelical song. Oliver A. Beckerlegge's and Frank Baker's commentary on Wesley's 1780 *Collection* (Wesley 1983) traces the tunes that Wesley suggested in the 1786 edition as appropriate for each hymn.

The life-long work of Frank Baker in Wesley hymnology, biography, and bibliography is crucial and noteworthy, particularly his *Representative Verse of Charles Wesley*, 1962, *Charles Wesley's Verse (An Introduction*, 2d. ed., 1988), and as Editor-in-Chief of *The Works of John Wesley*. Volume 7, *A Collection of Hymns for the Use of the People called Methodists*, 1780, edited by Franz Hildebrandt and Oliver A. Beckerlegge, was published in 1983. This work is the most comprehensive single-volume resource concerning the hymns and the musical references related to the 1780 *Collection*. Most subsequent commentary has been based to a large extent on the work of the scholars cited above.

The idea for this volume was suggested by the concluding remarks of Thomas A. Langford in his address "Charles Wesley as Theologian" to the Charles Wesley Colloquium (Princeton, NJ), September 22-24, 1989, where he made a strong case for the reunion of song and belief in United Methodist life and worship. The papers of that event are included in *Charles Wesley: Poet and Theologian*. During my research on Wesleyan music for the *Companion to The United Methodist Hymnal*, [1989] 1993, that idea was reinforced upon rereading Erik Routley's

*The Church and Music*, 1950, revised 1967, and his introductory chapters to *The Musical Wesleys*, 1968, on the musical activity and opinions of John and Charles. In the latter work Routley was the first to bring into one place and comment on a sampling of John's opinions in his *Journal*, occasional works, and correspondence, including his conclusion that John was "not in any sense a musician . . . having no use for music of the intellect" (Routley 1968, 22).

Little was evidenced in Routley's work or elsewhere concerning John's instinctive musicality, early musical training, and experiences that help account for his musical-editorial prowess and accountability that, combined with a publisher's aplomb, initiated and for half a century fostered and exploited the revival's vital musical-hymnic center. My research for a paper on John Wesley's 1737 Charlestown *Collection of Psalms and Hymns* presented to the Hymn Society in the United States and Canada, on July 9, 1990, Charleston, South Carolina, convinced me that it was for musical, pastoral, and pedagogical reasons that Wesley, as a young Anglican missionary priest in Georgia, adopted the texts in the collection into six iambic meters. I had not encountered this musical-pastoral side of John Wesley, and I suspected that a review of his work on his three tune collections might be rewarding and revealing. That work formed the core of my coverage of John Wesley.

Accounts of Charles's musical activity are almost exclusively restricted to his role as father and guide to the early training of organists and composers Charles Wesley, Jr., 1757-1834, and Samuel Wesley, 1766-1837. While most biographers note that Charles, unlike his brother John, moved and conversed with apparent ease among London's West End fashionable theater patrons and the significant composers of his day, Charles's musical sensitivities, vocabulary, and erudition, so far as I can determine, have not been brought into one place for examination. Except as the premier hymn writer of Methodism, Charles is seldom referred to, as is John, as the shaper of the revival's singing performance practice. This practice, a variant of a long-standing Anglican tradition, linked preaching with Methodism's societies, bands, and classes to proclaim and teach the faith to British audiences, and drew responses that ranged from enthusiastic acceptance to cool indifference or angry rejection  as anti-crown and anti-church.

I initially intended to include material on Charles and John Wesley and their contributions to the music of the Wesleyan revival as brief introductory chapters to my forthcoming book *Holiness & Hallelujahs: USA Church Music from a Wesleyan Perspective*, but the breadth and distinctly British setting of the Wesleys' activity prompted this separate volume.

The book's title, *Music of the Heart*, comes from the Charles Wesley hymn "Praise the Lord who reigns above" (**96** in *The United Methodist Hymnal*, 1989). In stanza two the poet characterizes  music as a heavenly art and "music of the heart":

> Celebrate th'eternal God
>     with harp and psaltery,
> timbrels soft and cymbals loud
>     in this high praise agree;
> praise with every tuneful string;
>     all the reach of heavenly art,
> all the powers of music bring,
>     the music of the heart.

The subtitle *John and Charles Wesley on Music and Musicians* suggests that both were creative, talented, opinionated, and productive in matters musical. The book is divided into two sections; the first is three introductory chapters: brief biographies of John and Charles Wesley; "Religion of the Heart" introduces the general discussion of religious affections with particular reference to John Wesley. This is followed by "Music of the Heart" and traces the significance of the embodiment of heartfelt religion in Wesleyan hymns and hymn singing.

Two major sections follow. The first concerns John Wesley as music editor and critic, including his work in Georgia where he compiled the 1737 Charlestown *Collection of Psalms and Hymns,* the three tune books, his "Thoughts on the Power of Music," with my commentary, "John F. Lampe, Methodism's First Composer," who set twenty-four theater-style tunes to Wesley texts in *Hymns on the Great Festivals*, 1746, and John's other opinions on music and music making.

The second, devoted to Charles Wesley, the poet of lyrical religion, includes excerpts about music, musicians, and hymns from his *Journal*, and his poetical commentary and opinions on music. The "Afterword:

Music of the Heart as Church Music" presents my evaluations and reflections on the Wesleys' "lyrical religion" and "music of the heart."

Page numbers in bold-faced type refer to hymns in *The United Methodist Hymnal*, 1989.

Many colleagues have encouraged me to write this book and have read the whole or portions, including Richard Watson, Professor of English, University of Durham and S T Kimbrough, Jr.,, President, The Charles Wesley Society, who have graciously supplied the preface and the foreword, respectively; Ivor H. Jones, Principal of Jesus College, Cambridge; Nicholas Temperley, the University of Illinois, Urbana; Robin A. Leaver, Westminster Choir College, Princeton, New Jersey; Kenneth E. Rowe, Methodist Archives, Drew University, Madison, New Jersey; Thomas A. Langford, Duke University; Frank Baker, Durham, North Carolina; and Jane Marshall and Lloyd Pfautsch, Dallas, Texas.

The volume's copyeditor, Sylvia Mills, who also copyedited *The Methodist Hymnal*, 1966, *Companion to the Hymnal,* 1970, and *Companion to The United Methodist Hymnal* [1989], 1993, has greatly assisted me in organizing a wide variety of material into a readable format. I also want to thank George H. Shorney, Chairman of Hope Publishing Co., for his support, perseverance, and good humor in seeing this project through.

I am grateful to the following for permission to include their material: Abingdon Press, *John Wesley's Sermons. An Anthology*, edited by Albert C. Outler and Richard P. Heitzenrater, © 1984, 1985, 1986, 1987, 1991 by Abingdon Press, and *The Works of John Wesley*, volume 18, *Journals and Diaries*, 1735-38, edited by W. Reginald Ward and Richard P. Heitzenrater, © 1988 by Abingdon Press; Frank Baker, *Representative Verse of Charles Wesley.* © 1962, and, *Charles Wesley's Verse, An Introduction*, © 1988; Gregory S. Clapper, *John Wesley on Religious Affections: his views on experience and emotion and their role in the Christian life and theology*, © 1989 by Gregory S. Clapper; and Nicholas Temperley, *The Music of the English Parish Church*, volume 1, © 1979 by Cambridge University Press;

Carlton R. Young
The Owl's Nest
Nashville, TN
November, 1994

1.  O for a heart to praise my God,
       a heart from sin set free,
    a heart that always feels thy blood
       so freely shed for me.

2.  A heart resigned, submissive, meek,
       my dear Redeemer's throne,
    where only Christ is heard to speak,
       where Jesus reigns alone.

3.  A humble, lowly, contrite heart,
       believing, true, and clean,
    which neither life nor death can part
       from Christ who dwells within.

4.  A heart in every thought renewed
       and full of love divine,
    perfect and right and pure and good,
       a copy, Lord, of thine.

5.  Thy tender heart is still the same,
       and melts at human woe:
    Jesus, for thee distrest I am,
       I want thy love to know.

6.  My heart, thou know'st can never rest,
       till thou create my peace,
    till of my Eden repossest,
       from self, and sin I cease.

7.  Fruit of thy gracious lips, on me
       bestow that peace unknown,
    the hidden manna and the tree
       of life and the white stone.

8.  Thy nature, gracious Lord, impart;
       come quickly from above;
    write thy new name upon my heart,
       thy new, best name of Love.

Charles Wesley, *Hymns and Sacred Poems*, 1742

# 1. John and Charles Wesley

*The Wesley Family*

"Wesley" originally was Welswe from the Somerset region in the mid-tenth century. It continued as Westley of Westleigh, Devonshire. The ancestors of John and Charles, many of whom were clergymen, lived in the west and south of England. The present spelling evolved through Wellesley, sometimes spelled Wesley, as in the instance of their grandfather, John, who was a controversial Anglican priest turned Nonconformist.

The following chart traces four generations of the better-known Wesleys:

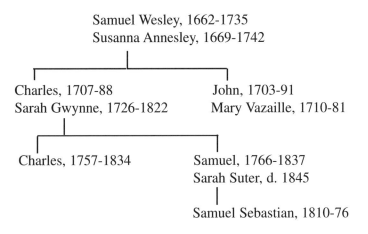

Samuel Wesley, 1662-1735
Susanna Annesley, 1669-1742

Charles, 1707-88
Sarah Gwynne, 1726-1822

John, 1703-91
Mary Vazaille, 1710-81

Charles, 1757-1834

Samuel, 1766-1837
Sarah Suter, d. 1845

Samuel Sebastian, 1810-76

**John Wesley** was born at Epworth, Lincolnshire, June 17, 1703, the son of the Anglican rector and former dissenter, Samuel, and the disciplining and indefatigable Susanna Wesley. Of the nineteen children born of the union, ten survived, seven girls and three boys. Martin Schmidt has commented on the convergence of traditions in the Epworth household:

It brought together the heritage of Puritanism, Anglican churchmanship, and that concern for the care of souls, social activity and missionary zeal, derived from the revival of the Religious Societies. At the same time it drew its sustenance from the Puritan culture of family life and from the nurture of individual souls found in Romanic mysticism. To this was joined the Halle type of pietism. Finally a place was given to liberal scholarship, and the harmonious, mystical piety of a Henry Scougal [*The Life of God in the Soul of Man*, 1677, an abridgment published by John in 1770] was held in high esteem. To this was added Susanna Wesley's personal gift as a teacher (Schmidt and Goldhawk 1962, 63).

When at the age of six John was dramatically pulled from a rectory fire, his mother believed that the boy's life was saved for God's purposes. John attended Charterhouse School and Christ College, Oxford, the latter conferring the B.A. in 1724 and the M.A. 1726-27, and was named a fellow of Lincoln in 1727.

Following his ordination in 1728 he became a curate to his father. The following year he returned to Oxford as a tutor, where he joined with Charles and others, including George Whitefield, in the activities of the Holy Club. In 1735 through the Society for the Propagation of the Gospel, John went to Savannah, Georgia, as a priest. During the journey and continuing in Georgia and later in England, John came in contact with the Moravians, whose influence and hymnody were to make a strong impression on his life and work. In Charleston he published the first English hymnbook meant to be used in worship, *A Collection of Psalms and Hymns*, 1737, an amazing collection of psalm paraphrases, English devotional poetry, English hymnody, and German hymns. His translations of German hymns, begun in Georgia, are the best of the eighteenth century; three are included in *The United Methodist Hymnal*, 1989:

Give to the winds thy fears (**129**)
Jesus, thy boundless love to me (**183**)
Thou hidden love of God (**414**)

Wesley's controversial ministry and an ill-fated love affair led to a warrant for his arrest. This combined with his feeling of abject failure as a missionary-priest prompted Wesley's unannounced departure for England in December 1737. In London he continued his faith-struggle mentored by the Moravian Peter Böhler. On May 24, 1738, while attending a meeting of evangelicals on Aldersgate Street, he heard the reading of Martin Luther's preface to the Epistle to the Romans and "felt his heart strangely warmed." Aldersgate, viewed from a perspective of Wesley's complex life-long spiritual journey and his ability to change his mind, remains a significant milestone rather than, as some maintain, a definitive style of conversion. See page 51.

During the summer of 1738 John visited the Moravians in Herrnhut. He returned disappointed with what he perceived as spiritual arrogance but impressed, as he was in Georgia, with their spirited song and the effectiveness of their bands and small devotional groups. Later that year in London he joined with Anglicans and Dissenters, including some of the former from the Oxford Holy Club, at the Fetter Lane meetinghouse where Moravian hymns were featured. Convinced he needed to form a distinctive evangelical witness, he purchased an old foundry building in London, converted it to a chapel, formed societies, and began to recruit lay preachers to found and care for Methodism's expanding mission. In 1744 he gathered his preachers into their first annual meeting; in 1784 with the "Deed of Declaration" it became the "annual conference," a distinctive institution of Methodism.

During his forty-three-year Methodist ministry Wesley traveled thousands of miles in England, Wales, Ireland, and Scotland, overseeing the movement and preaching wherever he was permitted in chapels, parishes, and the open field. John's enormous literary and publishing activity expressed his compelling pedagogical and pastoral instincts and, through the activity of the societies' book stewards, made reading and lay education synonymous with Methodism. His publications included a library of classics and devotional literature, translations, biblical commentaries, histories, sermons, diaries, journals, Charles's hymns in sixty-four collections, publications, and hymnbooks, and important for this study, three tune books. He died in London, England, March 2, 1791.

**Charles Wesley** was born in Epworth, December 18, 1707, the eighteenth child and youngest son of the Anglican priest Samuel and Susanna Wesley, and the brother of John. In 1716 he was enrolled in the Westminster School, London, with his room and board paid by his brother Samuel, an usher at the school. In 1721 he was elected a king's scholar and allowed free board and education. Obtaining a Westminster studentship, he studied at Christ Church, Oxford, where he received the B.A. in 1730 and the M.A. in 1732. It was in Oxford that he, John, George Whitefield, and others formed the Oxford Holy Club, modeled after Anglican groups promoting a disciplined approach to Bible study, worship, visitation to the sick and imprisoned, and the frequent observance of Holy Communion. Here the term "Methodist," describing those following a method of spiritual discipline, was born.

Shortly after Charles was ordained a deacon and priest in the Church of England in 1735, his brother John influenced him to go to the Georgia colony as a missionary, where he served as secretary to General James Edward Oglethorpe at St. Simon's Island and secretary of Indian affairs. In less than five months he became disillusioned and went back to England by way of Boston where he preached in several churches, including what is now Old South Church. After his return to England he became associated with William Law, Count Zinzendorf, and Peter Böhler, and was converted on May 21, 1738, Whitsunday, three days prior to his brother. It is significant that Charles's conversion, in contrast to his brother's, was life-changing (see pages 155-57), causing his consummate poetic and literary gifts to be expressed in what is thought to be his first religious verse: "Where shall my wondering soul begin" **(342)**.

While Charles is noted as the esteemed poet of the Wesleyan revival, he, no less than his brother, began, spread, and sustained the Methodist revival in Great Britain. In the 1740's Charles was a forceful preacher and a compelling organizer of the developing Methodist societies.

It was during those turbulent and formative times that he composed many of his most enduring hymns:

All praise to our redeeming Lord, 1747 **(554)**
And are we yet alive, 1749 **(553)**
And can it be that I should gain, 1739 **(363)**

Christ the Lord is risen today,  1739 **(302)**
Christ, from whom all blessings flow, 1740 **(550)**
Christ, whose glory fills the skies, 1740  **(173)**
Come, Holy Ghost, our hearts inspire, 1740  **(603)**
Come, O thou Traveler unknown, 1742 **(386)**
Come, sinners, to the gospel feast, 1747 **(339, 616)**
Forth in thy name, O Lord, I go, 1749 **(438)**
Hail the day that sees him rise, 1739 **(312)**
Hark the herald angels sing, 1739 **(240)**
Jesus, lover of my soul, 1740 **(479)**
Love divine, all loves excelling, 1747 **(384)**
O for a heart to praise my God, 1742 **(417)**
O for a thousand tongues to sing, 1740 **(57)**
See how great a flame aspires, 1749  **(541)**
Soldiers of Christ, arise, 1742 **(513)**
Where shall my wondering soul begin, 1739 **(342)**
Ye servants of God, 1744 **(181)**

In 1749 he settled in Bristol with his wife Sarah Gwynne. They had eight children; three survived, including Charles and Samuel  who were important early nineteenth-century musicians, and Sarah. In 1771 he and his family moved to Marylebone in London. Although Charles became increasingly distant from and critical of John's work, the two brothers remained very close. Charles regularly preached at the City Road Chapel, was involved in Methodist work, and continued to write. For several years he held subscription concerts in his home to promote his sons' careers.

Frank Baker comments that Charles Wesley's hymns are distinguished

> for their use of over forty-five iambic meters and in each of fifteen of them [he] wrote over a thousand lines of verse. The most prolific of all was his favorite form of six eights—8.8.8.8.88 rhyming ABAABCC. In this metre he composed over eleven hundred poems, a total of nearly twenty-three thousand lines, most of them with a vigour, a flexibility, yet a disciplined compactness, that proved this to be the instrument fittest for his hand (Baker 1988, 70).

Among the other unique qualities in his verse was his popularization of the anapaest.

> He was a pioneer in making it the medium for the irrepressible lilt of emotions which burst the bonds of conventional verse, as they did of conventional religion. (Baker 1988, 73)

Wesley's vast, experimental, lyrical, and subjective expression of the Christian experience prompted an expanded repertory of tunes, many appearing for first time in his brother's three tune collections.

Most noteworthy for evangelical song is his heavy reliance on scripture; for example in *Short Hymns on Select Passages of the Holy Scriptures*, 1762, he composed hymns and poems on every book of the Bible. His hymns are contained in sixty-four collections published in his lifetime. The collected works of Charles and John, compiled by George Osborn, comprise thirteen volumes, and there are over 1,000 unpublished poetical items in *The Unpublished Poetry of Charles Wesley*, compiled and edited by Oliver A. Beckerlegge and S T Kimbrough, Jr. See Frank Baker, *The Representative Verse of Charles Wesley*; Frederick Gill, *Charles Wesley, The First Methodist*.

Charles died in London, March 29, 1788. His life is summarized in this memorial in John Wesley's City Road Chapel, London:

> "God buries his workmen, but carries on His work."
> Sacred to the Memory
> of THE REV. CHARLES WESLEY, M. A.
> Educated at Westminster School
> And sometime Student at Christ-Church, Oxford.
> As a preacher
> He was eminent for ability, zeal, and usefulness,
> Being learned without pride,
> And pious without ostentation;
> To the sincere, diffident Christian,
> A son of Consolation;
> But to the vain boaster, the hypocrite, and the profane,
> A Son of Thunder.

He was the first who received the Name of  Methodist
And, uniting with his Brother, the Rev. John Wesley,
    In the plan of Itinerant Preaching,
Endured hardship, persecution, and disgrace
        As a good Soldier of Jesus Christ;
Contributing largely, by the usefulness of his labours,
To the first formation of the Methodist Societies,
            In these Kingdoms.

        As a Christian Poet he stood unrivalled;
And his hymns will convey instruction and consolation,
        To the faithful in Christ Jesus,
As long as the English language shall be understood.
  He was born the XVIII of December, MDCCVIII,
    And died the XXIX of March, MDCCLXXXVIII,
A firm and pious believer in the doctrines of the Gospel,
  And a sincere friend to the Church of England.

## 2. Religion of the Heart

Heart is a metaphor for a person's innermost character, feelings, or innermost part. It is the key word in the invitation and response: "Lift up your hearts [and minds]; we lift them up unto the Lord" that may have been a part of the Eucharist as early as the fourth century (Roberts and Donaldson 1873, 6)

It is also a perennial key word in pop music, e.g., "Young at heart," "With a song in my heart," "Peg of my heart" "I left my heart at the stage door canteen," "I left my heart in San Francisco," "Be careful, it's my heart," "This heart of mine," "My heart stood still," "Your cheating heart," and the country-western song "She stomped on my aorta."

Mary Elizabeth Mullino Moore notes that the metaphorical power of heart stems from its grounding in human physiology as "the center of the human body . . . [where it] cannot and does not function unilaterally, but in harmony with an intricate system of organs, regulatory mechanisms, vessels, and cells. . . . When we turn to the heart for a metaphor, then, we cannot be simplistic and deal with it as a separate entity apart from the brain or from any other part of the body. The heart is related to the entire body, continuously giving and receiving" (Moore 1991, 198-99).

Heart is used in four general ways in over 900 instances in 800 verses in Hebrew and Christian scripture. In rare instances it is a metaphor for the depths of the sea, "the deeps congealed in the heart of the sea" (Exod. 15:8), or the center of the earth, "For just as Jonah was three days and three nights in the belly of the sea, so for three days and three nights the Son of Man will be in the heart of the earth" (Matt. 12:40). It is more often used in the physical human sense: the center of physical vitality, e.g., "In the morning, when the wine had gone out of Nabal, his wife told him these things, and his heart died within him; he became like a stone" (1 Sam. 25:37); and "Jehu drew his bow with all his strength, and shot Joram between the shoulders, so that the arrow pierced his heart; and he sank in his chariot" (2 Kings 9:24); or the deepest levels of the human psyche, synonymous with "spirit" and "inward mind," as found in these passages from the Psalms:

Create in me a clean heart, O God,
and put a new and right spirit within me (Ps. 51:1).
(See Charles Wesley's hymn based on Psalms 51:1 at page xx.)

Therefore my spirit faints within me;
my heart within me is appalled (Ps. 143:4).

Who can search out our crimes?
We have thought out a cunningly conceived plot.
For the human heart and mind are deep (Ps. 64:6).

The heart is the place or the seat of the deepest human-felt and expressed emotion where a person expresses gladness: "Be wise, my child, and make my heart glad, so that I may answer whoever reproaches me" (Prov. 27:11), and "yet he [God] has not left himself without a witness in doing good—giving you rains from heaven and fruitful seasons, and filling you with food and your hearts with joy" (Acts 14:17); sadness: "So the king said to me, 'Why is your face sad, since you are not sick? This can only be sadness of the heart'" (Neh. 2:2); trouble (2 Kings 6:11); courage (2 Sam. 17:10); discouragement (Num. 32:7); fearfulness (Isa. 35:4); envy (Prov. 23:17); trust (Prov. 31:11); generosity (2 Chron. 29:31); or hatred (Lev. 19:17).

The heart is said to have failed (Gen. 42:28), to be faint (Gen. 45:28), to throb (Ps. 38:10), to tremble (1 Sam. 28:5), to be sick (Prov. 13:12) or broken (Ps. 69:20).

For Paul the heart was the source of both good and bad habits:

Therefore God gave them up in the lusts of their hearts
to impurity, to the degrading of their bodies among
themselves (Rom 1:24).

Brothers and sisters, my heart's desire and prayer to
God for them is that they might be saved (Rom. 10:1).

Recent studies have focused on the importance of the heart in understanding and expressing religious affections. Don E. Saliers in *The*

*Soul in Paraphrase* comments:

> To characterize the heart is to say what a human being is by calling attention to how the world is experienced and regarded . . . the heart as the seat of the affections *and* the understanding. . . . It gives us a way of speaking about what is deepest and most complex about human beings. . . . The language of faith is also the language of the heart (Saliers 1991, iv-v).

> Most central questions concerning life and death, love and hatred, or good and evil, require that we speak of these concerns in relation to how we are [daily] affected. That is why matters of moral and religious seem to the objective philosophical or scientific mind to be 'subjective'—precisely because they involve life as well as one's mind. To speak or to resolve 'with all one's heart' is therefore much richer and more concrete than making up our minds according to 'the principles of objective reason' (Saliers 1991, 19).

> The 'heart' is a place of conscience and moral capacity . . . [and] the concept of the heart then, not only explains what we do, it governs who we are (Saliers 1991, 20).

> *Almighty God, unto whom all hearts are open, all desires known, and from whom no secrets are hid: Cleanse the thoughts of our hearts by the inspiration of thy Holy Spirit, that we may perfectly love thee, and worthily magnify thy Holy Name, through Christ our Lord.*

> [In this ancient collect as we address God] as the one who knows the heart and thus the whole of our lives, we make clear what is believed in the very asking for purity of heart. . . the intention to love and praise God with one's whole heart and mind [and] to have the very life of God dwell in the believer (Saliers 1991, 23).

Corporate expressions of heartfelt faith and witness abound in the seventeenth and eighteenth centuries. Ted Campbell in *The Religion of the Heart,* comments:

> These religion of the heart movements . . . [while] concurring with older religious traditions in their belief that human beings in their "natural" state are separated from God, the religion of the heart movements maintained that this separation is overcome in affective ("heartfelt") experience: typically, in experiences of repentance (sorrow over sin) and faith (personal trust in God), but sometimes in more vivid experiences of personal illumination. The key element in their understanding of religious life, then, was their insistence that the "heart," denoting the will and affections (or "dispositions") is the central point of contact between God and humankind (Campbell 1991, 2-3).

The eighteenth-century Wesleyan revival is a distinctive heart movement with a unique theology—a heart repentant, assured, and forgiven; a heart overflowing in joyous response; a heart of love, and a heart of perfect intention.

Wesley discusses the changed heart in his sermons that he published in order to promote and explain the doctrines of Methodism. He often quotes Romans 5:5: "The love of God spread abroad in our hearts; for example, in "The Almost Christian," 1741, he asks, "Is the love of God shed abroad in your heart?" In the sermon "Original Sin," 1759, he states that the "great end of religion is to renew our hearts in the image of God" (Wesley 1991, 334).

Wesley states in "Upon our Lord's Sermon on the Mount IV," 1748, "Evidence of the changed heart, inward holiness, is in outward holiness, love of neighbor or social holiness:"

> It has been often objected that religion does not lie in outward things but in the heart, the inmost soul; that it is the union of the soul with God, the life of God in the soul of man; that outside religion is nothing worth; seeing God 'delighteth not in burnt offerings', in outward

services, but a pure and holy heart is the sacrifice he
will not despise.'

I answer, it is most true that the root of religion lies in
the heart, in the inmost soul; that this is the union of the
soul with God, the life of God in the soul of man. But if
this root be really in the heart it cannot but put forth
branches. And these are the several instances of outward
obedience, which partake of the same nature with the
root, and consequently are not only marks or signs, but
substantial parts of religion.

It is also true that bare, outside religion, which has no
root in the heart, is nothing worth; that God delighteth
not in *such* outward services, no more than in Jewish
burnt offerings, and that a pure and holy heart is a sacrifice with which he is always well pleased. But he is also
well pleased with all that outward service which arises
from the heart (Wesley 1991, 201).

In one of his earliest sermons, "The Circumcision of the Heart,"
1733, Wesley begins to form Methodism's most distinct teaching, "perfect love of God and neighbor, rooted in a radical faith in Christ's revelation of that love and its power" (Wesley 1991, 23).

No man has a title to the praise of God unless his heart
is circumcised by humility; . . . none shall obtain the
honour that cometh of God unless his heart be circumcised by faith, even a 'faith of the operation of God'
(Wesley 1991, 31).

Here then is the sum of the perfect law: this is the true
'circumcision of the heart.' Let the spirit return to God
that gave it, with the whole train of its affections. 'Unto
the place from whence all the rivers came, thither' let
them flow again. Other sacrifices from us he would not;
but the living sacrifice of the heart he hath chosen. Let
it be continually offered up to God through Christ, in
flames of holy love. . . . 'Set your heart firm on him, and

on other things only as they are in and from him.' . . .
'Have a pure intention of heart, a steadfast regard to his
glory in all your action' (Wesley 1991, 31-32).

In "The Law Established through Faith, II," 1750, Wesley discussed the role of faith in changing and purifying the heart.

> 2. This is therefore the main point to be considered:
> How may we establish the law in our own hearts so that
> it may have its full influence on our lives? And this can
> only be done by faith. Faith alone it is which effectually answers this end. . . . Faith . . . works inwardly by
> love to the purifying of the heart, the cleansing it from
> all vile affections. Everyone that hath this 'faith,' 'in
> him purifieth himself, even as he is pure'—purifieth
> himself from every earthly, sensual desire, from all vile
> and inordinate affections; yea, from the whole of that
> carnal mind which is enmity against God. At the same
> time, if it have its perfect work, it fills him with all
> goodness, righteousness, and truth. It brings all heaven
> into his soul, and causes him to walk in the light, even
> as God is in the light (Wesley 1991, 284).

In the sermon "The New Birth," 1760, Wesley states that God
speaks to the heart of the man (those) who have been 'born again,' 'be
of good cheer, thy sins are forgiven thee' . . . [and] he 'feels in his heart'
(to use the language of our Church) 'the mighty working of the Spirit of
God' [and is] conscious of, a 'peace which passeth all understanding.'
He many times feels such a joy in God as is 'unspeakable and full of
glory'. He feels 'the love of God shed abroad in his heart by the Holy
Ghost which is given unto him'. . . God is continually breathing, as it
were, upon his soul, and his soul is breathing unto God. Grace is
descending into his heart, and prayer and praise ascending to heaven.
And by this intercourse between God and man, this fellowship with the
Father and the Son, as by a kind of spiritual respiration, the life of God
in the soul is sustained: and the child of God grows up" (Wesley 1991,
339-40).

Wesley refers to religion of the heart in "The Way to the Kingdom,
1746: "While true religion naturally leads to good word and work yet

the real nature thereof lies deeper still, even in 'the hidden man of the heart.' "

> 6. I say of the *heart*. For neither does religion consist in *orthodoxy* or right *opinions*; which, although they are not properly outward things, are not in the heart, but the understanding. . . . He may be almost as orthodox as the devil (though indeed not altogether; for every man errs in something, whereas we can't well conceive him to hold any erroneous opinion) and may all the while be as great a stranger as he to the religion of the the heart.

> 7. This alone is religion, truly so called: this alone is in the sight of God of great price.

> 10. True religion, or a heart right toward God and man, implies happiness as well as holiness. For it is not only righteousness, but also 'peace and joy in the Holy Ghost.'

> 12. So soon as ever he [God] takes unto himself his mighty power, and sets up his throne in our hearts, they are instantly filled with the 'righteousness, and peace, and joy in the Holy Ghost' (Wesley 1991, 125, 126, 131).

In the sermon, "Upon our Lord's Sermon on the Mount, IV," 1748, Wesley discusses the role of the heart in outward and inward religion.

> It is most true that the root of religion lies in the heart, in the inmost soul; that this is the union of the soul with God, the life of God in the soul of man. But if this root be really in the heart it cannot but put forth branches. . . . It is also true that bare, outside religion, which has no root in the heart, is nothing worth; that God delighteth not in such outward services, no more than in Jewish burnt offerings, and that a pure and holy heart is a sacrifice with which he is always well pleased. But he is also well pleased with all that outward service which arises from

the heart; with the sacrifice of our prayers (whether public or private), of our praises and thanksgivings; [and] with the sacrifice of our goods (Wesley 1991, 201).

In one of his last sermons, "On living without God," 1790, Wesley describes the work of the Holy Spirit upon the heart:

But the moment the Spirit of the Almighty strikes the heart of him that was till then without God in the world, it breaks the hardness of his heart, and creates all things new. The Sun of righteousness appears, and shines upon his soul, showing him the light of the glory of God in the face of Jesus Christ. He is in a new world. All things round him are become new. Such as never before entered into his heart to conceive. He sees, so far as his opened eyes can bear the sight,

The opening heavens around him shine,
With beams of sacred bliss (Wesley 1991, 568).

I believe the merciful God regards the goodness of the heart rather than the clearness of the head; and that if the heart of a man be filled (by the grace of God, and the power of his Spirit) with the humble, gentle, patient love of God and man, God will not cast him into ever-lasting fire prepared for the devil and his angels because his ideas are not clear, or because his conceptions are confused. Without holiness, I own, no man shall see the Lord; but I dare not add, or clear ideas (Wesley 1991, 572).

In the sermon "Catholic Spirit," 1750, Wesley uses the image of the heart in what has become one of his most important statements about the nature of the church universal:

If thine heart is as my heart, it thou lovest God and all mankind. I ask no more: Give me thine hand (Wesley 1991, 306).

Wesleyan piety, religion of the heart, is unique in several important ways that are identified by Gregory S. Clapper in *John Wesley on Religious Affections: his views on experience and emotion and their role in the Christian life and theology:*

> The heart [for Wesley] is the locus for God's action in the human . . . (Commentary on Romans 8:27) [and] a connection between the heart and the senses . . . through the hardness of their hearts—-callous and senseless. "And where there is no sense there can be no life" (Eph. 4:18). . . . The heart is not stable and indelible but can change over time. . . (Clapper 1989, 46, 47).

> When the grace of God had changed his [Wesley's] heart, . . . he was the fitter instrument to serve God's wise and merciful purposes in the defense and propagation of Christianity. . . (Clapper 1989, 49).

> Wesley often links "spirit" and "soul" with the heart . . . [when] describing the integration of self to render him the most intelligent and sincere, the most affectionate and resolute service (Clapper 1989, 51).

> [Wesley] on Jesus's affections: "[They] were not properly passions, but voluntary emotions, which were wholly in His own power. And this tender trouble, which He now voluntarily sustained, was full of the highest order and reason" (Clapper 1989, 54-55).

Clapper invented the term "orthokardia" to describe Wesley's vision of Christianity "which cannot be conveyed by stressing only beliefs or actions, yet neither is it conveyed by focusing on self-contained inner states or 'feelings.' Without such a 'right heart,' there is no Christianity on Wesley's terms" (Clapper 1989, 154).

> Opposing both rationalism (Christianity as assent to correct beliefs) and so-called pietist (Christianity as a mat-

ter of felt experience), Wesley aimed to show that theological integrity and a rich emotional life are not inconsistent with each other. His aim was, in fact, to show that these two require each other (Clapper 1989, 164)

The simple message of the Gospel [could] change hearts and lives without requiring the believer to be a post-graduate student in theology. . . .Wesley showed that the affections were much more than what they are commonly regarded to be, that is, inner states which are a source of error and confusion or which only confound the so-called 'higher faculties of reason and understanding.' Wesley showed that if the seeker after truth was not humbly filled with love and joy about what God had done for him or her, then the Gospel message had not really been heard and Christianity had not yet taken root in that person's life. . . .The religious affections work in concert with the reflective mind, not against it (Clapper 1989, 158-59, 161).

The gracious affections . . . pattern and orient the self. God's atoning work is the object of these affections, and (through the confirmation and strengthening of the sacramental ministry of the church) they become dispositions to behave, dispositions to do those works of love and mercy which the compassionate heart perceives to be needed (Clapper 1989, 164-65).

The Wesleys uniquely paraphrased and presented the religion of the heart in song—the music of the heart—a song of hope, new life, wholeness, and peace for rich and poor alike. They raised hymn singing to a distinctive religious art form so that John Wesley could characterize hymns and hymn singing in his remarkable preface to the 1780 *Collection*, as the "handmaid of piety" and a means of raising or quickening the spirit of devotion, confirming faith, enlivening hope, and kindling and increasing our love for God and the human family.

# 3. Music of the Heart: Lyrical Religion

> Just as theology prevents music from becoming an end
> in itself by pointing man to its origins—in the doxology
> of creation, music prevents theology from becoming a
> purely intellectual matter by moving the heart of man to
> consider its ultimate purpose—the doxology of the new
> creation (Robin Leaver, *Duty and Delight, Routley
> Remembered*, 49).

The joining of belief and praise with music is evident in Greek and
non-Western cultures. Hebrew Scripture, particularly the Psalms, contains numerous hymns of praise and faith, including creation and
enthronement hymns. The latter psalms were of special interest to the
early Christian church because of their messianic content.

There are at least six categories of early Christian hymns in the New
Testament (see page 4 in *Companion to The United Methodist Hymnal*).
Gnostic-Hellenistic hymns date from the second century of the common
era, Judeo-Hellenistic hymns from the third century, and Syrian-
Hellenistic hymns from the sixth century (Werner 1959, 221-26).
Ambrosian and monastic hymns date from the fourth century, and the
latter flourished in the tenth to the sixteenth centuries.

Geoffrey Wainwright has commented on the roles of hymns and
hymn singing in Christian worship:

> St. Augustine's definition has found wide acceptance. It
> looks for the combination of three characteristics: a
> hymn is *praise;* it is praise *of God*; it is the *sung* praise
> of God. . . . The praise of God must be sung, but the
> variety of the literary and musical forms is great. . . .
> Moreover, the "balance" in the singing between the

word element and the music element is quite variable: sometimes the word will so predominate as to make the singing little more than rhythmic speaking; sometimes the musical elaboration will outweigh the verbal content. . . . [The] best "congregational hymns" . . . achieve an admirable balance between the two. Singing is at home in the liturgy because worship bears, in Christianity as in other religions, the character of *dromenon,* a complex "drama" of words and actions in which music may help to bring mental and physical activity together in unity or counterpoint. . . . Singing clearly demonstrates worship—and therefore the divine kingdom and human salvation—to be an affair of the whole person, mind, heart, voice and body. . . . Singing is the most genuinely popular element in Christian worship. . . . [It unites] the whole assembly in active participation to a degree which is hardly true of any other component in the liturgy (Wainwright 1980, 199-200).

Ivor H. Jones comments that congregational song

unites the intellect, the emotions, the will and the voice in a human response to God's grace. . . . The emotions find particular resonances in music and the freedom is found there to make new commitments and acts of will . . . [within] the unity of singing together. . . . Far from being just the handmaid of the words it is the music which enables the total hymn, words and music, to be an authentic story of what we believe and who we might become (Jones 1990, 151-52).

### Martin Luther

For Protestants, the integration of belief and song has roots in the fifteenth-century movement known as the Bohemian Brethren, founded by the reformer Jon Hus, 1369?-1415, who advocated that scripture, its teaching, and preaching should be in the language of the people, and worship centered in the common cup and in the singing of hymns. In Germany a century later, Martin Luther, 1483-1546, dilettante musician, articulate writer, translator, and preacher, embodied that reform in the *chorale*: unison strophic-form melodies composed from traditional and liturgical sources set to vernacular paraphrases of biblical and liturgical texts.

Carl Halter and Carl Schalk have commented on Luther's views on music:

> For Luther, music was next in importance to theology, a living voice of the Gospel (*viva vox evangelii*), a gift of God to be used in all its fullness in Christian praise and prayer. . . . [Luther], alone among the reformers of the 16th century, welcomed music into the worship and praise of God with open arms. For Luther, music was a "noble, wholesome, and joyful creation" (Halter and Schalk 1978, 15).

According to Carl Schalk, Luther's hymns joined doxa (praise), and logia (words) in proclamation:

> Early Lutheran hymnody [was] a vigorous proclamation of doxological texts which spoke the "Good News" plainly and directly, and associated with melodies which attempted to match in their vigor and rhythmic strength that same proclamation (Glover 1990, 298).

Carl Schalk comments on the relationship of the congregation, choir, and organ in early Lutheran worship:

> When the congregation sang the growing body of vernacular hymns, it did so in unison and unaccompanied. The choir's function in connection with the hymns was to present polyphonic settings (such as those in Johann Walter's collection of 1524) in alternation with the stanzas sung by the congregation. The organ did not accompany the congregation as is customary today, but presented intonations to the liturgical chants and often alternated with the singing in the presentation of certain chants such as the Introit, Kyrie, and Magnificat (Halter and Schalk 1978, 63).

The chorale tradition developed for almost two centuries and culminated in the devotional hymns of Paul Gerhardt, 1607-76: "Jesus, thy boundless love to me" **(183)** (translated by John Wesley); others in English translations: Johann Franck, 1618-77, "Deck thyself, my soul, with gladness" **(612)**; Martin Rinkart, 1586-1649, "Now thank we all our God" **(102)**; and Johann Heermann, 1585-1647, "Ah, holy Jesus, how hast thou offended" **(289)**; and the hymns of the Pietistic movement, 1675-1750. This seventeenth-century hymn repertory formed the core of J. A Freylinghausen's collections *Geistreiches Gesangbuch*, 1704, and *Neues Geistreiches Gesangbuch*, 1714, that greatly influenced Moravian hymnody. See pages 58-59.

### *The Influence of John Calvin*

A second stream of Reformation hymnody, metrical psalmody, was developed by John Calvin, 1509-64, in his attempt to reform Christian worship in strict conformity to New Testament norms: prayer, preaching, and praise. Calvin's repertory of congregational song was initially limited to metrical paraphrases of the 150 psalms set to rhythmic unison melodies, sung without accompaniment. He later included paraphrases of the Lord's Prayer, the Song of Simeon, the Ten Commandments, and the Summary of the Law.

Walter Blankenburg comments on Calvin's views on music:

> He had no feeling at all for the developing art of sacred music. He was conscious of the significance of instruments in the Old Testament (he evaded their mention in the New Testament, Ephesians 5:19), but he considered their use in the worship service there only as a preliminary to a more perfect divine service in the New Testament, only "puerilia elementa" for which Christians no longer had any need. He was guided to this decision by the opinion that only music directly bound to a text and understandable by the congregation was justified in the service. Unison, unaccompanied congregational singing in the vernacular thus became the only form of service music (Blume 1974, 517).

Calvin's two-decade collaboration with poets Clement Marot, ca. 1497-1544, and Theodore de Bèze, 1519-1605, and composer, editor, and arranger Louis Bourgeois, ca. 1510-ca. 1561, and others, resulted in over thirty psalters, some with tunes. A selection from these works was published as the *Genevan Psalter*, 1562, including 125 tunes in 110 different meters (Reynolds and Price 1987, 29-32).

While Calvin's radical worship reforms excluded choirs and instruments from worship, the 1562 *Genevan Psalter* tunes were harmonized by Claude Goudimel, ca. 1520-72, and set in motet form for three, four, or more voices. Composers in France and Netherlands used the tunes in settings for instruments and voices, and "the sixth and seventh decades of the 16th century produced a whole series of other polyphonic editions" (Blume 1974, 536).

Metrical psalmody was introduced to England by Thomas Sternhold in *Certayne Psalmes chose out of the Psalter of David . . .* , ca. 1547, and by Anglican clergy exiled to Frankfurt and Geneva during the reign of Mary I, 1553-58, who brought it and other ideals of continental Reformed worship to England and Scotland (See Robin A. Leaver, *Goostly Psalmes and Spirituall Songes*). Early psalters include the Anglo-Genevan Psalter, 1560-61; Thomas Sternhold and John Hopkins, *The Whole Book of Psalms Collected into English Meter*, 1652, often called "The Old Version"; John Day, 1522-84, *English Psalter*, 1563; William Damon, ca.1540-ca.1591, *The Psalmes of David*, 1579; Thomas Est, ca. 1540-ca.1608, *The Whole Booke of Psalmes*, 1592.

The poetry was of uneven quality, most of it set in common meter (CM) 86.86, a form adapted from the Old English ballad meter known as "fourteener." Other psalms were cast in short meter (SM) 66.86, a variant of common meter, and long meter (LM) 88.88, taken from the Genevan Psalter and the Latin office hymn. Beginning with Day's *Psalter*, 1562, a section in the front of many collections included instructions on singing and note reading.

Seventeenth-century psalters include Thomas Ravenscroft, ca. 1592-ca. 1635, *The Whole Book of Psalmes*, 1621, with a generous supply of tunes including OLD 100TH (75) from the *Genevan Psalter*, the

*Scottish Psalter*, 1635, with 144 tunes, and Nahum Tate, 1652-1715, and Nicholas Brady, 1659-1726, *A New Version of the Psalms of David*, 1696, with a tunes *Supplement*, 1708, the latter with several standard tunes including HANOVER (181) and ST. ANNE (117). EASTER HYMN (302) is the sole surviving tune from *Lyra Davidica*, 1708, an anonymous collection of translations of German and Latin hymns with tunes. Other early eighteenth-century tune books are by Henry Playford, 1623-86, *Divine Companion*, 1701, that included UFFINGHAM (450), John Bishop, 1665-1737, *A Set of New Psalm-Tunes*, 1710, and William Tans'ur, 1706-83, *A Compleat Harmony of Syon*, 1734.

### *Hymns and Hymn Singing*

Myles Coverdale, ca. 1488-ca. 1569, was the first to introduce the Reformation hymn, and presumably hymn-singing, to England in *Goostly Psalmes and Spirituall Songes*, ca. 1535, a collection of forty-one hymns, including thirty-six translations of German texts, with tunes. In 1546 the collection was condemned heretical and was burned. The only other hymn collection of the sixteenth century was apparently the eight *Primer* hymns, 1545; Robin A. Leaver has commented that these hymns were "unlike the translations from office hymns found in earlier English primers, [that] were obviously intended for devotional reading, . . . [these] could easily have been sung [and probably were] to their associated plainchant melodies, even though the *Primer* was issued without notation (Glover 1990, 366).

For over 150 years the church almost exclusively used metrical psalms. In spite of this practice and the official prohibition of hymn writing and hymn singing, hymns were appended to seventeenth-century editions of Sternhold and Hopkins. These texts included metrical versions the of Veni Creator, biblical songs, the Te Deum, prayers and hymns. George Wither, 1588-1667, published without official permission a hymn collection *Hymns and Songs of the Church*, 1623, and spent some time in jail for his efforts. Orlando Gibbons composed tunes for this collection. Hymns were included in other psalters, including John Cosin's paraphrase of Veni Creator, "Come, Holy Ghost our souls inspire" **(651)** in John Playford, *The Whole Book of Psalms*, 1677.

Playford's *Psalms and Hymns*, 1671, is apparently the first collection in which psalms and hymns are interspersed. There were also private collections of religious poetry such as *The Temple* by George Herbert, 1593-1633, in the eighteenth century adapted as hymns, e.g., "Let all the world in every corner sing" **(93)**. Occasional hymns were composed and presumably sung, including Thomas Ken's "All praise to thee, my God, this night" **(682)**.

Robin A. Leaver comments that psalms as well as hymns were sung in high church Anglican societies that were established in the latter part of the seventeenth century to promote a corporate devotional life:

> Some societies produced their own devotional handbooks that included a small selection of hymn texts together with modest collections of tunes—all taken from the familiar English psalm tune tradition (Leaver 1994, 1).

The hymns of dissenter poet-preacher Isaac Watts, 1674-1748, "When I survey the wondrous cross" **(298)**, were models of simplicity. Frank Baker comments that Watts, though "capable of much more in the way of lyrical experiment . . . restricted nine-tenths of his production to the three common iambic forms" [CM, SM and LM, see page 58] (Baker 1988, 70). His hymns were meant to be sung by his congregation on first hearing, using the psalm tunes that they had memorized. The hymns were apparently taught in the traditional lining-out style of parish psalm singing.

Robin A. Leaver comments on the style of Watts's hymns:

> Watts ignored the accepted form of slavish Scriptural paraphrase and instead wrote in a soaring poetic style, Scriptural in content but all-embracing in scope, that forever changed the direction of English congregational song, liberating it from the strait jacket of metrical psalmody (Glover 1990, 378).

Reynolds and Price make this evaluation of Watts:

> Watts is called the father of English hymnody not because he vastly improved or reformed the hymns that were already being written in his day, nor because of any radical change in form or structure. It is because he produced a "new song" based on the experiences, thought, feelings, and aspirations common to all Christians, expressed in what might be called classic objectivity. . . .[He wrote hymns] that would illustrate, reenforce, and climax the sermon from the pulpit. . . . Sermon and hymn emerged together, but the hymn remains long after the sermon has been forgotten (Reynolds and Price, 1987, 47-48).

Frank Baker comments that the English evangelical hymn that was born in Watts's hymns "can be distinguished from related species of verse . . . by reference to four criteria, two concerned with its content and two concerned with its form":

> 1. It is *religious*, an act of worship.
> 2. It is communal in its approach to religion, containing sentiments which may shared by a group of people, even though they may all be expected to sing 'I' instead of 'we'.
> 3. It is *lyrical*, written to be sung, not chanted or intoned.
> 4. It is comparatively *regular* both in metre and in structure, and consists of at least two stanzas.

> If all four elements are not present to a marked degree, then it would be better to speak of the composition by some specific name appropriate to its special function, such as anthem, chant, chorus, doxology, or else (to use Charles Wesley's own term) as a 'sacred poem' (Baker 1988, 90-91).

*Methodism: A Lyrical Religion of the Heart*

James F. White has characterized the eighteenth-century British Wesleyan revival and its worship life as a

> countercultural movement in the midst of the English Enlightenment . . . [that was] denounced for producing Spirit-filled Christians or "enthusiasts" rather than staid pewholders [and] reached out primarily to the poor . . . in an era that placed so much emphasis on power and prestige. . . . To reach the poor urban masses [of Bristol, Birmingham, and London], one had to go beyond the parish system and develop a whole new form of mission. This outreach shaped Methodist worship in definite ways (White 1989, 152).

Much of the Wesleys' early activity occurred in urban Anglican parishes whose worship life, Nicholas Temperley comments, was

> a mere introduction to a sermon, in which reason, allied to carefully chosen biblical texts, was used to justify conventional morality, charity and good works, and the existing order of church and state. Little thought was given to the emotional and spiritual needs of common people (Temperley 1979, 100).

The Wesleyan revival was also a heartfelt reaction to and an identification with the struggle of the vast majority of the population of Great Britain to exist in "an age when social structures were rapidly changing, when traditional beliefs had been challenged, and when moral improvement had become, for many people, the very essence of religion" (Campbell 1991, 102). The revival's wealth of affection in cultic and public expressions, and for this study its congregational song, was a welcome alternative to a cold and formal religion that seemed indifferent to and removed from everyday life.

Fred D. Gealy has commented, "Concurrent with preaching salvation, universal love, perfection, justification by faith, and assurance the Wesleys [and their revival, brought] into existence two kinds of hymns, the evangelistic hymn and, following Isaac Watts's pioneer and paradigmatic work, the hymn of Christian experience" (Gealy, Lovelace, Young 1970, 32). See also "And can it be that I should gain" (**363**) and "Come, O thou Traveler unknown" (**386**). For commentary on these hymns see pages 156-61.

The Wesleys uniquely paraphrased the religion of the heart into song, proclaiming their version of the good news of salvation in Jesus Christ in a singable and memorable idiom. S T Kimbrough, Jr. is the first scholar to identify this union of music and poetry as "Lyrical theology."

> *Lyrical theology* then is a "sung" theology, or at least a theology expressed in poetry and song. This means the mode of expressing what we so often are accustomed to hear and see in prose comes to fruition in a different world of language (Kimbrough 1994, 19).

Kimbrough further characterizes lyrical theology, after Walter Brueggemann, as world-making: "In the moment of speech and imagination the person awakes, embraces, and experiences a new world" (Brueggemann 1988, 12), a theology of sound, "made for the ear, lips, body, the senses," not bound by time and space, [so that it] may move through time without linear chronology and celebrates belief without dissecting it. . . . Lyrical theology helps us in faith to hold the paradoxes and inconsistencies of life in balance without subjecting them to theological logic and without translating theological affirmations into canons of belief" (Kimbrough 1994, 32, 38).

An additional feature of lyrical religion is the reinforcement of belief through the experience of recall. In this recall, religious experiences that time and reflection have divided into categories of mind and heart, thought and feeling, are rejoined and reinforced through preaching, prayer forms and hymn singing.

Lyrical theology, hymn singing, is dependent upon the informed, active, and full participation of each person in the congregation. In Wesleyan-style congregational song each is informed through study and rehearsal; the compelling music prompts the memory and the imagination, as well as the kinesthetic response, so that all move with and within the music; and the tune is so memorable and compelling that it invites others to sing.

Frank Baker has commented that because of their heartfelt and transforming conversion experiences Charles and John Wesley

> were profoundly convinced that a personal experience of God's saving and sustaining love was possible not only for an elect few, but for all men. . . . Salvation must be "free," but it must also be "for all"; otherwise it was hardly a gospel. Both became keynotes of Methodist preaching and Methodist singing (Baker 1988, 16).

The religion of the heart practiced, preached, and taught by the Wesleys and their itinerate lay-preachers proclaimed that God does not condemn persons to poverty, ignorance, and powerlessness. The enormous energy that emanated from each person's changed, informed, and disciplined heart was the wellspring for the revival's enormous energy and missional action in the name of Jesus Christ—the heart changed from cold indifference to warm affection—and prompted and guided persons to engage and recruit others in bold acts of compassion and reconciliation.

T. S. Gregory comments on the confidence implicit in Wesleyan hymns and hymn singing:

> Moreover, he [Charles Wesley] is confident—and this conditions all his poetry—that what he sing, prays and proclaims is valid, not for himself only or all Englishmen, but for 'all mankind', and this 'mankind' is

not the theologian's abstraction of human nature, or a contemporary convention of 'society' or the average Englishman or the common lot of mortals, but every soul of man for whom *my* Saviour died (Gregory 1958, 255).

One of the most remarkable aspects of Wesleyan hymns is that they were sung by divergent people in varying levels of theological understanding in a variety of religious, social, and economic settings, reflecting the revival's central theme of salvation for all in Christ. Ivor H. Jones comments, "They were intended to take folk from their youngest days to their death bed" (Jones 1990, 137). An important reason for their wide acceptance was that they tended "to rely on metaphors of clarity rather than of allusion [and] . . . that particular use of metaphor encourages a serious wrestling with the text, rather than only a personal adaptation of it" (Jones 1990, 132).

The Wesleys also used singable melodies (see pages 92, 102, 120) in a variety of styles to foster the memorization, recall, and reinforcement of a hymn's message that enlivened one's faith story.

> With the addition of a musical element a further area of interpretation comes into view. Everyone knows how a set of words can shift its meaning with a different musical setting. Charles Wesley's hymn "And can it be" sung to a boisterous and rhythmically insistent tune such as *Sagina* is a very different hymn from "And can it be" sung to the stark *Jena* or the more thoughtful and pliant *Didsbury.* . . . Hymns are open and, to a degree, adaptable, and they are adaptable both because of the character of the text and the character of the music. They adjust to our story. They allow us room for reflection. Our theology emerges as we present them as part of our account of ourselves. [In singing Wesley hymns] our story is also open to the hymn. We can listen, absorb and, given time and opportunity, internalize what the hymn is about (Jones 1990, 131-33).

By the close of their half-century evangelical revival the Wesleys had published sixty-four collections of hymns and three collections of tunes, and had established the unity of word and song as the vital center of worship and preaching for commitment. Methodist class meetings used the singing, recitation, and study of hymns to form a member's faith and prayer, and through tonal memory to inform, recall (anamnesis), and sustain between preaching services their faith in the saving power of God in Christ. Other hymns were sung in homes and evangelical chapels as solos using collections such as *Hymns on the Great Festivals,* set in 1746 by John F. Lampe, a bassoonist in the Covent Garden orchestra, celebrated composer, and a Wesley convert (see pages 105-10).

Albert C. Outler has commented:

> The brothers Wesley set great store by the fact that their people *sang* the same doctrine in their hymns as they heard and read in their sermons. Accordingly, the most copious source of quotations in the written sermons [John's], besides the Scripture itself, is from the succession of hymn collections provided for the Methodist people. Here, Charles's contribution to the Revival was unique; far more of his hymns have been sung by more Christians (and not just Methodists alone) than any sermon of John's has ever been read (Wesley 1984, 102).

According to Oliver A. Beckerlegge,

> Hymns played an important part in all the additional means of grace developed by the Methodist societies— the bands, the class-meetings, the love-feasts, the watch-nights, the prayer meetings, the covenant services. Almost every gathering began and ended with a hymn, and the class-meeting especially became a kind of family circle (Wesley 1983, 65).

Thomas A. Langford of Duke Divinity School has commented that the Reformed tradition's "reasoned word" was transformed by Wesley into the "sung word"; that is, it was characterized by singing hymns and songs of assurance, grace, pardon, and witness set to memorable music. "Just as in medieval times when stained glass was the acceptable way to convey words, actions, events, and personages of the faith, in the Wesleyan tradition the means for transmitting the faith is primarily the congregation's song replete with the gospel message" (Conversation with Carlton R. Young, September 1993).

The next two chapters trace the development of the music of the heart in the work and witness of John and Charles Wesley.

# 4. John Wesley: Tune Book Editor and Music Critic

### Musical Interests

John Wesley's musical experiences began with psalm singing, led by his mother Susanna in the Epworth rectory, and hearing the parish choir begun by his father Samuel, rector from 1696 to 1735, as early as 1702 (Temperley 1979, 143). The Parish Church of St. Andrew, the building dating from the thirteenth century across the meadow from the rectory, is the dominant feature of the environs. It is accessed from the village of Epworth by walking up a stone-flagged pathway overhung with lime trees. John recalls as a youth the clerk leading his homegrown introduction to the Te Deum:

> One Sunday, immediately after sermon, my father's clerk said, with an audible voice, "Let us sing to the praise and glory of God, an hymn of mine own composing." It was short and sweet, and ran thus:—
>
> King William is come home, come home!
> King William is home to come!
> Therefore let us together sing
> The hymn that's cal'd Te D'um.
> (Wesley 1984,10:445)

His musical experiences continued as a student singing psalms in worship at Charterhouse School, where he spent six years. At Christ Church, Oxford, where he lived for fifteen years including his early days in the Holy Club, Wesley learned, led, and sang Watts's metrical paraphrases using the tunes in the 1708 musical supplement to the Tate and Brady psalter, and other collections; see pages 2-3. Frank Baker comments that Wesley had a "uniform devotion to the singing of psalms and hymns as a daily and even hourly part of his own spiritual life . . . [and he] practiced singing four or five times a day" (Baker and Williams 1964, vi). According to Curnock, "With the exception of prayer and conversation, no word occurs more frequently [in the *Journal* and *Diary*] than singing" (1938, 114).

Wesley also played the flute. Richard P. Heitzenrater in an unpublished lecture, "Things seen and not seen—the world of Wesley's Diary," comments that Wesley's daily routine in his early twenties included practicing the flute (Heitzenrater 1993). Later in Georgia, Wesley recorded in his *Journal* for May 5, 1737, "played upon the flute"; and for May 18, "played upon the flute from 8:50 until 9:15(pm)." John L. Nuelson comments that "his (Wesley's) musical abilities did not go beyond playing the flute, by which means he taught others the tunes he had heard by the Germans" (Nuelsen 1972, 26, 66). Wesley apparently left his flute behind when he departed Savannah, and it was returned to him during the post-Aldersgate meeting in Oxford by Charles Delamotte, who had recently returned from Georgia ("House Warming" by G. Elsie Harrison, 1939, for the bicentennial of the Bristol New Room).

### John Wesley's 1737 Charlestown Collection of Psalms and Hymns

Wesley's first hymnbook, *Collection of Psalms and Hymns*, 1737, was compiled in Georgia while he was an Anglican missionary-priest. Wesley embarked for Georgia on the *Simmonds* October 14, 1735, "accompanied by three companions: his brother Charles, his friend Benjamin Ingham, and the son of a London merchant, Charles Delamotte" (Schmidt and Goldhawk 1962, 135). Two months were spent moving slowly, sometimes during fierce storms, off the east coast of Kent, past St. Helen's harbor and Yarmouth and in the Bay of Biscay awaiting a suitable and sustained wind. Wesley was deeply moved by the spirited singing of the Moravians' *Singstunde* (singing hour). His numerous references in his *Journal* to singing or song while on board the *Simmonds* begin October 19, "sang with Germans," and continue throughout the voyage. Two days earlier he had started German grammar "in order to converse with the [twenty-six] Moravians onboard," and on October 27 he began to study the Freylinghausen *Gesangbuch* (Wesley 1988, 10:137).

The 1737 *Collection* was prepared for, but apparently not used beyond, the parish (now Christ Church in Savannah) that stretched from Savannah down the coast to Frederica.

> The congregation which awaited John Wesley presented a motley appearance. It included Anglicans and Dissenters, although its direction was definitely in the hands of Anglicans, a position which was strengthened by their appointing a clergyman. As to its personnel, groups and individuals of very varied types belonged to it. In the first place there were debtors, mostly poor, but on the whole steady characters, although some were easy-going spend-thrifts and swindlers. Then there were avowed adventurers and work-shy types who could not settle into any order, as well as folk who had made a shipwreck of their lives and who were now intent upon making a fresh start (Schmidt and Goldhawk 1962, 156-57).

Frederick C. Gill comments that

> Frederica was a little more than a place on the map, a wretched outpost of Empire, as yet poorly organized, con-sisting of a fort, huts and tents, with only its storeroom for a church and no other facilities for pastoral work. The sur-rounding territory was a wilderness of wood, swamp and prairie, of prowling and thieving Indians and wild life. Georgia itself was a small strip of country between South Carolina and Florida, as yet unparcelled out, with a sea coast of sixty or seventy miles. Savannah was a town of frame-work houses (Gill 1964, 52).

After his return to England Wesley provided twenty-eight fascinat-ing paragraphs of impressions and descriptions of primitive Georgia's terrain, waterways, vegetation, climate, and people (Wesley 1988, 195-204).

Wesley's "Georgia experience" was characterized by (1) his relationship with the Moravians that continued on his return to England, culminating in his so-called Aldersgate "experience"; (2) his disappointment in failing to be the first to convert the Indians (a flashback to St. Paul converting the heathen?), finding instead that French missionaries had preceded him by a century; (3) his ill-fated love-affair with Sophy Hopkey, and (4) as a hard-working parish priest, as seen in the schedule of his last Sunday in the Savannah parish, demonstrating his consummate energies as well as his acquired linguistic abilities:

> MP 5-6:30
> Italian prayer at 9
> HC and Ser 10:30-12:30
> French prayers, psalms and scripture at 1
> Catechizing of children at 2
> Evening Prayer, 3
> House meeting, reading, prayer and praise until 8
> Attended Moravians at 9

Baker documents some of the unique characteristics of Wesley's ministry in Georgia that were later applied in the Methodist movements in Great Britain and the USA: hymn singing in the Eucharist, extemporary prayer, itinerate preaching, preaching without notes, utilizing the services of laypersons including women he called deaconesses, and organizing societies for religious fellowship that functioned apart from stated and ordered public worship (Baker 1970, 51).

We do not know the print quantity of *A Collection of Psalms and Hymns*, how it was transported from the printer in Charlestown to Savannah, Wesley's intended use in his parish, nor its fate after Wesley's departure. Presumably a few copies found their way into the colonies, and others were taken to England possibly by Wesley. His first hymnal was eclipsed and all but lost within the great mass of popular hymnody that he proliferated during Methodism's rapid expansion in the eighteenth century and sustained by his followers, both in England and the USA, well into the nineteenth century. Two copies were discovered in the late nineteenth century, and they have provoked significant discussion, clearly showing that (1) the *Collection* is a unique eighteenth-century USA bibliographic artifact, and (2) its content and organization point toward the kind and quality of "Methodist" collections published by Wesley during the next half century, culminating in 1780 with *A Collection of Hymns for the Use of the People called Methodists.*

A reprint of the *Collection* was included by George Osborn in *The Poetical Works of John and Charles Wesley*, 1868-72, and Richard Green discussed it in *The Works of John and Charles Wesley, A Bibliography* (1906). John Julian in *Dictionary of Hymnody* (1907, 726) provided a brief article. James T. Lightwood, cited by Williams in *John Wesley's First Hymn Book* (Baker and Williams 1964), provided additional bibliographical information. In the USA Winfred Douglas in *Church Music in History and Practice*, 1937, and Leonard Ellinwood in *The History of American Church Music*, 1953, described its importance for USA hymnic bibliography. Robert Stevenson in *Patterns of Protestant Church Music*, 1953, devoted a chapter to it, which was reprinted in Baker and Williams' 1964 work. Their work, the most complete documentation and discussion of Wesley's *Collection*, is divided into four sections.

The first section is a chapter from Robert Stevenson's work in which he links the multifaceted activities of Wesley, the young Anglican missionary priest in Georgia, February 6, 1736, to December 24, 1737, to the circumstances of the first hymnal compiled, printed, bound, and used in America and intended for use in public worship (see Stevenson 1953). The second section contains the *Collection*'s seventy psalms and hymns. The third section contains the pioneer work of Frank Baker, "The Sources of John Wesley's *Collection of Psalms and Hymns*, Charleston, 1737," a study he prepared for the 1958 meeting of the Wesley Historical Society and in which he documents the sources of all but one of the seventy selections in the *Collection.*

Baker begins with a listing of the sources, many of which Wesley either took with him or were available in Savannah, and then provides not only the source of each selection, but also valuable comments on the way that the editor, without a revision committee, let not one text stand as the poet had written it, but cut stanzas and changed words and whole phrases. Wesley changed all the texts from whatever foot and meter the poet had written into 6 basic meters, all iambic in some combinations of

6's and 8's. For instance, Wesley changed George Herbert's "O King of glory, King of Peace," trochaic 74. 74., into "King of Glory, King of peace," iambic CM, and for good measure he tacked on to the end of the reconstructed text two lines from Addison's "When all thy mercies."

The fourth section by George Walton Williams discusses the physical properties of the *Collection*, which had been printed by Lewis Timothy, a former associate of Ben Franklin. Timothy (Timothée), the son of a French protestant refugee, left France, learned printing in Holland, and came to Philadelphia, where he was first employed by Ben Franklin in his printing house; he later served as librarian of the Philadelphia Library Company. He moved to Charleston in 1733, took over the print shop of Thomas Whitmarsh, successor to Eleazar Phillips (both died in less than two years of establishing their presses), changed his name to Timothy, began publishing a newspaper in 1734, and printed material for the government. He died in 1738.

Williams declares improbable Stevenson's suggestion that Wesley during his first trip to Charleston, August 3, 1736, left the edited copy of the *Collection* with Timothy and that he returned to read proof eight months later, April 18, 1737. Timothy would have had to lock up his modest supply of type in one project for about eight months (1964, xx). Williams also reviews the circumstances of the acquisition of two extant copies of the *Collection*, the first in London, 1878, by W. T. Brooke; the second in 1899 by the New York Public Library. The whole work could hardly have been proofed at any one time, since its content was in process for well over a year. The primitive conditions of travel and the absence of domestic mail service probably caused Wesley to forward to Timothy, via messenger, the balance of the proofing after he, Wesley, had on April 18, 1737, approved matters of basic format and design. See pages 43-44. Either Timothy or an associate (perhaps his son Peter who took over the business at his father's death in 1738) is responsible for the bulk of the final corrected copy, including the twenty-two textual errors and several others in formatting. For additional discussion on the printing of the *Collection* see Martha W. England, "The First Wesley Hymn Book."

Until the work of Baker and Williams, commentary on the *Collection* was incidental to the coverage of Wesley's failed ministry where he was usually portrayed as the great "hymnic" innovator who got into deep trouble and had to skip the country. The record suggests, however, that the "innovator" moved ever so cautiously, proving the contents of the *Collection* for over a year within the parish life of Savannah and Frederica.

When the Grand Jury received the twelve complaints, it dismissed those dealing with "hymns and psalms," presenting instead ten true bills, all of which are critical of Wesley's leadership in matters liturgical concerning his performance of the priestly office, not hymnological. Among them: dividing Sunday worship into three gatherings: 5:00 a.m.; 9; Communion and Sermon, 11:00-12:30; and Prayer again at 3:00, which he defended as "according to ancient practice."

Two of the original 12 grievances (public charges) presented to the Savannah Grand Jury by the chief magistrate, Charles Causton (Sophy Hopkey's uncle), on August 22, 1737, concerned Wesley's use of hymns and psalms in worship, and any discussion of the importance of the *Collection* of necessity must deal with them. Number 2 reads: "By altering such passages as he thinks proper in the version of the psalms, publicly authorized to be sung in the church"; number 3,"by introducing into the church and service at the altar compositions of psalms and hymns not inspected or authorized by any proper judicature"; and number 4, "By dividing the Morning Service on Sundays." Charges 2 and 3 were dropped when the majority of the Grand Jury, which reviewed the 12 charges, formed its 10 true bills.

The additional complaint (number 3) about Wesley's leadership in liturgy, but not sustained in the true bills, should be mentioned in any discussion of *A Collection of Psalms and Hymns* since it has to do with the singing of hymns and psalms, presumably from the *Collection* during the distribution of Holy Communion. This practice was apparently borrowed by Wesley from the Moravian love-feast noted in his *Journal* for June 8, 1736, the same day a warrant was issued for him to be taken into custody:

> After Evening Prayers we joined with the Germans in
> one of their Love-feasts. It was begun and ended with
> thanksgiving and prayer, and celebrated in so decent and

solemn a manner as a Christian of the apostolical age would have allowed to be worthy of Christ (Wesley 1988, 537).

Wesley is apparently unique in his generation of Anglican clergy for a consummate knowledge and applied use of German in his translations. He also introduced German tunes from *Lyra Davidica*, 1708, and Jacobi's *Psalmodia Germanica*, 1722, and "the Freyinghausen Hymn Book, in which melodies were attached, a copy of which he had got hold of in Georgia" (Nuelsen, Parry, Moore, and Holbrook 1972, 12-14; 65).

Frank Baker comments on number 3 of the original complaints, Wesley's use of hymns "at the altar."

> As we have seen in Georgia, Wesley added hymns to the communion office, and this practice became even more helpful in the crowded and therefore protracted English services; short hymns or groups of stanzas were sung during communion of the people as a devotional background for their movements to and from the communion rail (Baker 1970, 86).

Wesley as priest, poet, and editor, beginning in the spring of 1736 and continuing for about a year, apparently used every opportunity to test the contents of the *Collection*. Curnock has commented:

> An analysis of the Diary would show that the discovery, translation and alteration of a hymn was accompanied by frequent singing. In private devotions, public worship, society meetings, at the bedside of the sick, he sang the psalms and hymns which formed the *Collection* and the collections of 1739, 1740 and 1741 (Savannah, October 28, 1736). He sang also with his communicants' class after evening exposition. Did he sing Brevint's sacramental hymns or Hickes, or his father's 'Behold the Saviour of mankind'? Any of these is possible. In Savannah, for the

present, the communicants' class seems to have taken the place of the society-meeting. . . . Hymn by hymn the *Collection's* quality was tested by use (Curnock 1938, 269, 269 n).

### *Journals and Diaries*

The following excerpts from John Wesley's *Letters*, 1980, *Journal and Diaries*, 1988, three journals and three diaries, some  appearing for the first time, construct a sequence for Wesley's work during 1736-37 on the *Collection*, and his other hymnic and musical activity in Georgia. "Sang," private and with others, is  entered almost every day, many times early in the morning and before going to sleep, often with multiple entries for the day, and usually combined with prayer or meditation. "Sang with Germans," "German," "German grammar," "Translated German," and "with Germans" appear throughout the text. The most obvious references to preparing the *Collection* are entries "Translating," "Transcribing," "Read Proof," or "Reading Hymns," the latter private and with others. Entries simply "Verse" are included, and although the meaning is presumed to be Wesley writing hymns, the entry is unclear. There are also numerous entries "Sang with boys." Presumably these boys were sons of members of the Savannah parish with whom Wesley often talked,  catechized, walked, and even felled trees! There are two references to Wesley playing the flute. Capitalizations are as they appear in the text. If the word is lowercased, it is usually part of a fuller entry for the hour. The number preceding the entry, e.g., "9 Translated Psalms," is the hour of the day.

Work on the *Collection* began early in 1736, intensifying in December and continuing into the New Year. Since the project and sequence of the *Collection* were complex, with  over 2,000 lines of poet-ry, Wesley apparently from time to time sent copy to and received proofs from the printer via messenger. In April he probably brought with him proofs that he had not returned to Charleston, left them with Timothy, who had operated a noted print shop there since 1733, and read new proofs.

Wesley's hymnic activity culminated in June and July of 1737. The entries may have been one or combinations of the following: proofing pages from the *Collection*, teaching hymns to his parish from the printed *Collection*, or writing and editing hymns that were not included in the *Collection*, activity he resumed the following year in England.

# 1736

**FEBRUARY 23**. 9 Translated German Psalms.

**MARCH 5**. 7 Revised Prayerbook. 8 Revised Common Prayer book. 9 Looked over psalm book. 10 Psalm book. 12 Ended psalm book. **19**. 1:15 With Germans and read psalms.

**MARCH 15**. [Wesley's earliest translation of a German text is found in a letter to Count Zinzendorf. It is a translation of stanza 13 of Freylinghausen's "Wer ist wohl, wie du, Jesu süsze ruh?" that Wesley had heard in Moravian worship in Savannah and included as a hymn at page 39 in his *Collection*.]

> A patient, a victorious mind,
> That, life and all things cast behind,
>    Springs forth, obedient to thy call,
> A heart that no desire can move,
> But still t'adore and praise and love,
>    Give me, my Lord, my life, my all.
>                          (Wesley 1980, 449n)

**MAY 5**. 3 Translated German psalms. **22**. 9:30 Transcribed verses.

**JUNE 10**. We began to execute at Frederica what we had before agreed to do at Savannah. Our design was, on Sundays in the afternoon and every evening after public service, to spend some time with the serious of the communicants in singing [probably Watts's metrical paraphrases], reading, and conversation. . . . After the psalm and a little conversation, I read Mr. Law's Christian Perfection and concluded with another psalm. **14**. 10 Translated German.

**JULY 2, 7, 8, 9**. Translated verses. **17, 19**, Writ verses.

**AUGUST 14**. 1 Read Collection to Miss Sophy. **28**. 9 Transcribed hymns. **31**. 9 Transcribed verses. 6 Marked Psalms and Hymns.

**SEPTEMBER 7**. 4 Read *Collection*.

**OCTOBER 18**. Finding there were several Germans at Frederica who, not understanding the English tongue, could not join in our public service, I desired them to meet at noon in my house, which they did every day at noon from thenceforward. We first sung a German hymn, then I read a chapter in the New Testament, then explained it to them as well as I could. After another hymn we concluded with prayer and the Blessing.

**DECEMBER 18**. 11:15 [and 4:30] Scheme for psalms. **19**. 1 Scheme for hymns. **20**. 7 Scheme for hymns. 9 Transcribed hymns. **21**. 7:30, 8, 4 Hymns. **22**. 7, 8:30, 11 Hymns. **24**. 7, 8 Hymns. 12 transcribed hymns. 1, 6 Hymns. **25**. 7, 8 Hymns. **26**. 4, 8 hymns. **27**. 4, 7, 9 hymns.

## 1737

**JANUARY 15**. 9 Watts's hymns. 12 Watts's Psalms. 2 ended Psalms. **16**. 5, 9, 12, 4:15 6 Watts. **17**. 3:15, 5, 8, 11:30, 12:45, 3, 6, 7:45 Watts. **18**. 5, 6, 7:30, 12 Watts. 1:30, 8 Hymns. **19**. 5, 6, 8, 1:15 Hymns. **20**. 8, 11:45 Hymns.

**FEBRUARY 25**. 9 Writ hymns. 10 Hymns.

**FEBRUARY 26**. [In a letter to Thomas Bray's Associates in the S.P.G, London Wesley describes his activity with small groups parish:]

Some time after the evening service as many of my parishioners as desire it meet at my house (as they do also on Wednesday evening) and spend about an hour in prayer, singing, and mutual exhortation. A smaller number (mostly those who design to communicate the next day) meet here on Saturday evening; and a few of these come to the other evenings, and pass half an hour in the same employment (Wesley 1980, 495).

**MARCH 17**. 8 transcribed hymns. 9, 10 Hymns. **22**. 8 verse; sang. 9 Made verse; sang; 10 Verse; sang. 11 Verse; writ them. 12 Writ them. 2:45 Transcribed. **23**. 8, 4:30 verse. **24**. 4:30 hymns. **26**. 6:30 Hymns. **27**. 7:15 Hymns. 12:45 Hymns. **28**. 5 Read hymns.

**APRIL 2**. 7 transcribed verses for Miss Sophy. **4**. 7 Transcribed (hymns) journal. **6**. 12:15 Read hymns. **14**. [Charleston] 8 Necessary talk with Mr. Timothy. [Printer of *Collection*. **18**. 5 transcribed hymns. 6 Hymns. 9 corrected proof. **19**. 9 [visited] Mr. Timothy's.

**MAY 5**. 9 [pm] Played upon the flute. **18**. 8:50 [pm] Played the flute.

**JUNE 4**. 1:15 [wrote] verses. 5 verses. 9 Writ verses. **6**. 3:30 Writ verse. **10**. 7 [pm] Verses. **13**. 5:30 Verse. 7 Verses. **17**. 7 Verse. 8 Verse. 9 Verse. 1 verse. **19**. 4:30 Verse. **24**. 2 Watts. 3 Watts. **25**. 7:30 verse. 8 verse. 10 Verse. 6 Verses. **26**. 8 writ verse. 9 writ verse. **28**. 9 Collected hymns. 10 Hymns. **29**. 8 Verse. 9 [pm] verse. **30**. 8 Verse. 9 writ verse. 8 Verse. 2 Writ verse. 4 writ verse. 8:45 Verse.

**JULY 6**. 6:15 verse. 7 Verse. 11 Verse. 12:20 Writ verse. **8**. 9 Writ verse. **13**. 6 Writ hymns. 7:30 Hymns. 8 Hymns. 9 hymns. **14**. 6:15 Hymns. 10 Hymns. 12:45 Hymns. 1 hymns. 2:45 Hymns. 3:30 Hymns. **15**. 6:15 Hymns. 9 hymns. 10 Hymns. 10:30 hymns. 11:30 Hymns. 12:30 Hymns. 4:40 Hymns. **16**. 6:30 Hymns. 9:45 Hymns. 2 Hymns. **19**. 6 hymns. 7 Hymns. 1 Hymns. 3 Hymns. **20**. 6 Hymns. 8 hymns.9 Hymns.12:30 Hymns. **21**.10:15 Hymns.

**AUGUST 18**. 8 Gesangbuch.

Wesley's efforts to blend English and German repertory began with this collection, the first hymnbook, compiled and printed in the USA and intended for use in Anglican worship. Wesley's experimental use of the *Collection* reflects the work-style of missionaries who join the indigenous with the imported and the improvisational and tentative with the informed and timely. Half a century later Wesley invoked this same attitude when he provided the American societies with hymns, psalms, an abridged prayer book and ordained leaders.

Martha England reminds us that besides demonstrating Wesley's skill in bringing together a wide variety of texts, the *Collection*

> is perhaps most important in its revelation of the duties of an editor of hymn books. [As for Wesley's penchant for altering texts] . . . the result of insistence upon absolute purity of text would be to end one of the lives of some great hymns, and relegate them to rare book rooms, where the pure texts live another quieter life (1964, 237).

The seventy selections in the *Collection* are organized in three sections after the *Book of Common Prayer*.

> Sunday, 3-39: forty selections of general praise;
> Wednesday and Friday, 40-58: twenty selections for fast days;

> Saturday, 58-74: ten selections of praise to God the Creator of all things.

Frank Baker describes the *Collection* as a

> pioneer attempt at grafting hymn-singing on to the
> *Book of Common Prayer* [that] was a presage of one of
> the outstanding features of the Methodist Revival, and
> was not without influence in Anglican worship (Baker
> 1970, 47).

Wesley also took on the task of setting the *Collection* to music, a task so far as this writer is aware that no one has either examined or documented. This writer discovered this facet of Wesley's work on the *Collection* quite by accident while reviewing Baker's work (1964, xxvii-xxxiv). Baker traces the sources of 69 of the 70 texts, occasionally making some comment about Wesley's alteration of a text from one meter to another, even taking the German texts from their original meter and translating them in another. After reading all of Baker's comments in this regard, this writer then went through the entire *Collection* and catalogued each text according to its meter. The pattern soon was clear: Wesley had brought all the texts in the *Collection* into conformity with 6 meters, all variants of 8's and 6's, all iambic (see page 47). Line by line, some 2,000 in all, from manuscript pages he shaped the texts by singing the tune he felt appropriate, teachable, singable, and memorable, beginning with the tunes he could remember singing in the Epworth rectory family circle and at Christ Church, and more recently the German chorales he heard the Moravians singing during the journey to Georgia.

Wesley's numerous references in his *Journal* to singing or song while on board the *Simmonds* begin October 19, "sang with Germans," and continue throughout the voyage. Two days earlier he had started German Grammar "in order to converse with the [twenty-six] Moravians onboard," and on October 27, 1735, he began to study Freylinghausen's *Gesangbuch* (Wesley 1988, 137 ). See pages 33-34 for a discussion of Wesley's life-long interest in music, an interest documented in his *Journal* and *Diary* that according to Curnock shows "with the exception of prayer and conversation, no word occurs more frequently in the [*Journal* and *Diary*] than singing" (Curnock 1938, 114).

Wesley made each of the *Collection's* 2,000 lines of text, with few exceptions, conform to six meters, CM, SM, LM, LMD six 8's and twelve 8's. Wesley's editorial work is illustrated at number 20, page 21, in the 1737 *Collection*, where he changed Herbert's trochaic 74.74 to iambic CM (86.86).

> King of Glory
> King of Peace,
> I will love thee

is changed to

> O King of Glory,  King of Peace,
> Thee only will I love;

In the following chart the number in parenthesis indicates the frequency of use of each meter in the *Collection's* hymns for Sunday, Wednesday and Friday, and Saturday.

| CM (86.86) | | 6 8's | |
|---|---|---|---|
| SU (40) | 17 | SU (40) | 7 |
| WF (20) | 9 | WF (20) | 0 |
| SA (10) | 0 | SA (10) | 1 |
| **Total** | **26** | **Total** | **8** |

| SM (66.8.6) | | 8's | |
|---|---|---|---|
| SU (40) | 3 | SU (40) | 0 |
| WF (20) | 4 | WF (20) | 0 |
| SA (10) | 2 | SA (10) | 1 |
| **Total** | **9** | **Total** | **1** |

| LM (88.88) | | LMD (88.88.88.88) | |
|---|---|---|---|
| SU (40) | 12 | SU (40) | 0 |
| WF (20) | 7 | WF (20) | 0 |
| SA (10) | 4 | SA (10) | 3 |
| **Total** | **23** | **Total** | **3** |

What English or German tunes, presumably suitable, singable, teachable, and memorable, did Wesley use during the twelve months as he apparently tested the contents of the *Collection* and other translations from the German and altered English hymns, later published in England?

Some tunes no doubt were sung for the first time anywhere in the New World. While we do not know which tunes, the tunes that Wesley used were probably selected using these criteria: those in the 6 basic meters in common use in England in the early eighteenth century; and those most likely learned and sung in Epworth; Christ Church, Oxford; the Holy Club; and from the Germans on board the *Simmonds*.

The following tunes, which may have been used by Wesley in Savannah to teach the selections in the 1737 *Collection,* are referenced to the *Foundery Collection*, 1742, his first tune collection. See pages 54-56 for additional information about their sources.

Common Meter

ST. MARY'S TUNE, *Foundery Collection,* 1742, page 13; its present form is from Playford's *Whole Book of Psalms,* 1677; an earlier form is in Edmund Prys's *Psalter,* 1621; it was sung to "On God supreme our hope depends," page 4 in the 1737 *Collection,* a text, according to Baker, Wesley had begun to revise as early as 1726 (Baker and Williams 1964, xxviii).

BURFORD, *Methodist Hymn Book,* 1933, page 193, called "St. John's" in *Foundery Collection,* page 14; its earlier form may have been the tune used with Samuel Wesley's "Behold the Saviour of mankind," in the 1737 *Collection,* page 47. Tradition has it that the hymn by the elder Wesley was saved along with young "Jacky" from the 1709 Epworth rectory fire.

Short Meter

WIRKWORTH, *Methodist Hymn Book,* page 364; *Foundery Collection,* page 13; sung to two texts: "O throw away thy rod," in the

1737 *Collection,* page 45; and "Come, ye that love the Lord," in the 1737 *Collection,* page 8; the latter is a text in every Methodist collection of hymns since its introduction in the 1737 *Collection.*

### Long Meter

TALLIS' CANON, page 642, *Hymns and Psalms,* 1983, and page 42 in the *Foundery Collection,* may have been used by Wesley in Georgia, evidenced by his inclusion (see the final stanza, the 1773 *Collection,* page 11) of the familiar doxological stanza:

> Praise God from whom all blessings flow
> praise him all creatures here, below;
> praise him above, ye heavenly host,
> praise Father, Son and Holy Ghost.

This stanza is from Bishop Ken's morning and evening hymns, "Awake, my soul, and with the sun" and "Glory to thee, my God, this night," in 1674 published in his manual of prayers for the students of Winchester College. According to Watson and Trickett (1988, 367), Tallis' tune first appeared in Matthew Parker's *Whole Psalter translated into English Meter*, 1561-67, and the texts, ca. 1674, were not sung to TALLIS' CANON until the eighteenth century. Wesley could have learned both the tune and the texts at either Epworth or Christ Church, Oxford.

Wesley may have used TALLIS' CANON for the Watts text "Praise ye the Lord: tis good to raise," page 10, in the *Collection.* Stanza 1, lines 3 and 4, often quoted by Erik Routley, became the title of his colleagues' commemorative volume, *Duty and Delight*:

> His nature and his works invite
> to make this duty our delight.

A second LM text from the *Collection,* page 51, is a translation from Richter, "Thou Lamb of God, thou Prince of Peace"; this can be sung to TALLIS' CANON and WINCHESTER NEW, *Hymns and Psalms*, page 84. The latter is called SWIFT GERMAN, *Foundery Collection*, page 34, and was probably abridged in Georgia by Wesley from a tune he adapted from Freylinghausen's *Gesangbuch,* 1704.

### Six 8's

VATER UNSER, *Foundery Collection,* page 33, a familiar tune to the Moravians, was probably known by Wesley prior to his time in Georgia, and he may have matched it to two texts in the 1737 *Collection:* "O Jesu, source of calm repose," 38, and "I'll praise my maker," (did Charles in "Thou hidden source of calm repose," 1749, borrow the first line of the former?).

"I'll praise my Maker" might also have been sung to OLD 113TH (ES SIND DOCH SELIG ALLE) from *Strassburger Kirchenamt,* 1525 (see number 23 in *Hymns and Psalms,* 1985), provided the stanzas were doubled. More likely, though, Wesley set it to "Ye priests of God, whose happy days," as he did in *Foundery Collection,* page 35. It remains a mystery who abridged OLD 113TH to make it "the American tune" for the four-stanza hymn "I'll praise my Maker." Wesley was apparently very fond of this hymn and included it in his final *Collection,* 1780, recommending in the 1786 edition for it to be sung to "113th Psalm." The preface to *The Methodist Hymn Book,* 1933, states that Watts's hymn was "on Wesley's lips as he lay dying, and its message is one of the heirlooms of Methodism."

Most studies about the *Collection's* hymnic importance, i.e., its uniquely broad content, particularly the first substantive connection of German and English hymnody, tend to understate the pastoral, liturgical, and musical contexts in which it was conceived, its contents processed, and its use in parish worship.

Wesley's efforts to produce a collection of inclusive congregational song not only resulted in the first of its kind intended for use in Anglican worship, but demonstrates the way that evangelical hymnals ought to be constructed to insure their initial and continuing use. Wesley also shows that a basic principle of hymnal editing should be to make hymnals more, not less, accessible and therefore useful to the audiences for which they are meant to serve as a means of sung prayer and praise.

In preparing the *Collection* Wesley demonstrates his sensitivity to the pastoral-musical dimensions of hymnody as he selected, translated, and reduced the *Collection's* seventy selections, including psalm paraphrases, English devotional poetry, and his translations from the German into six iambic meters, CM, SM, LM, LMD, six 8's and twelve 8's, for ease of teaching. He is thought to have played his flute to teach the tunes.

By making all the texts conform, either through selection or alteration, to six basic meters so that they could be sung, Wesley's innate musical sensitivity and intelligence were first tested and applied. In his struggle to match texts with tunes Wesley saw the pastoral need to standardize tunes and print them in cross-referenced tune books: the *Foundery Collection*, 1742, *Sacred Melody*, 1761, and *Sacred Harmony*, 1780.

> In Georgia, Wesley not only initiated his fifty-year career as text editor and publisher of hymnals, but by testing the contents of his first hymnal as to their singability he began his parallel activity of compiling and publishing tune books and initiated that compelling aspect of the Wesleyan ethos, "singing what was preached, and preaching what was sung" (Young 1993, 48).

### John Wesley's Conversion

John's conversion, the so-called "Aldersgate experience," occurred on May 24, 1738. It was first included in his *Journal* published in 1740, which covered this time-frame. The entry for May 24 begins in paragraph 13 of his extended preface to the events of that day.

> I think it was about five this morning [Wednesday, May 24, 1738] that I opened my Testament on those words: [Greek text follows] 'There are given unto us exceeding great and precious promises, even that ye should be partakers of the divine nature.' Just as I went out I opened it again on those words, 'Thou are not far from the kingdom of God.' In the afternoon I was asked to go to St.

Paul's. The anthem was 'Out of the deep have I called unto thee, O Lord. Lord, hear my voice. O let thine ears consider well the voice of my complaint. If thou, Lord, wilt be extreme to mark what is done amiss, O Lord, who may abide it? But there is mercy with thee; therefore thou shalt be feared. [. . .] O Israel, trust in the Lord: For with the Lord there is mercy, and with him is plenteous redemption. And he shall redeem Israel from all his sins' [Psalm 130:1-4, 7-8, *Book of Common Prayer*].

14. In the evening I went very unwillingly to a society [see Wesley 1988, 249n] in Aldersgate Street, where one was reading Luther's Preface to the Epistle to the Romans. About a quarter before nine, while he was describing the change which God works in the heart through faith in Christ, I felt my heart strangely warmed. I felt I did trust in Christ, Christ alone for salvation, and an assurance was given me that he had taken away *my* sins, even *mine*, and saved *me* from the law of sin and death.

15. I began to pray with all my might for those who had in a more especial manner despitefully used me and persecuted me. I then testified opening to all there what I now first felt in my heart. . . .

17. Thursday, May 25. The moment I awakened, 'Jesus, Master, was in my heart and in my mouth; and I found all my strength lay in keeping my eye fixed on him, and my soul waiting on him continually. Being again in St. Paul's in the afternoon, I could taste the good word of God in the anthem, which began, 'My song shall be always of the loving-kindness of the Lord: with my mouth will I ever be showing forth thy truth from one generation to another' [Psalm 89:1, *Book of Common Prayer*] (Wesley 1988, 249-50).

Wesley's conversion was essentially a change of heart, as seen in his four distinct references: "describing the change which God works in the heart," "I felt my heart strangely warmed," "what I now first felt in my heart," and "Jesus, Master, was in my heart and in my mouth," (see chapter 1, "Religion of the Heart").

For our study it is important to note that Wesley's conversion was in part prefaced during evensong in St. Paul's Cathedral as the choir sang a setting of Psalm 130. As Martin Schmidt comments:

> The words of the anthem, which Wesley wrote out in full in his *Journal*, were from Psalm 130: "Out of the deep have I called unto Thee, O Lord." It may well have been sung to the setting of W. [William] Croft [1678-1727] which was published in 1742, and which by constant repetition emphasized the words: "Trust in the Lord" (Schmidt and Goldhawk 1962, 1:262).

Erik Routley has commented on the presumed musical setting:

> The impressive thing about this [Croft's] setting is that it opens with a solo, highly expressive, and exactly what John later confessed appealed to him most (Routley 1968, 27).

On the following two days Wesley returned to St. Paul's for evensong and was again strengthened as the choir performed psalm settings of hope and trust.. On Thursday he heard Psalm 89:1, and on Friday, Psalm 62:1-2, 8. According to J. Joseph Wisdom, Librarian, St. Paul's Cathedral, and Stephen Freeth, Keeper of Manuscripts, Guildhall Library, the composers of these settings and Psalm 130 that Wesley heard on Wednesdy, can not be determined because there is no information in Cathedral records about the choral settings sung at evensong on these dates. (Correspondence with Carlton R. Young, October 1994)

John's conversion experience was preceded three days by his brother's on Whitsunday, and the brothers shared in the debut of Wesleyan evangelical song. On 24th May, John Wesley's heart was "strangely warmed," and Charles uniquely records in his *Journal:* "Towards ten, my brother was brought in triumph by a troop of our friends, and declared, 'I believe.' We sang the hymn [was the tune CRUCIFIXION TUNE, 706 in *Hymns and Psalms*?] with great joy, and departed with prayer" (Baker 1962, 3).

### John Wesley's First Tune Book

John Wesley's first tune book is *A Collection of Tunes, Set to Music, As They are commonly sung at the Foundery*, 1742, usually called the *Foundery Collection* (Reprint 1981, Bristol, England by Bryan F. Spinney). There are thirty-three tunes arranged by meter.

Here Wesley brings together English and German melody for the first time in any substantive way, reflecting in part the tunes he used in Georgia to teach the hymns and psalms in the 1737 *Collection;* for example, his father's text "Ye priests of God, whose happy days" at page 5 in the 1737 *Collection*, in the *Foundery Collection* is set to OLD 113TH psalm tune, a match that may have begun in Georgia.

The tunes are presumed to be the favorites of Wesley and the society gathered for worship in the abandoned cannon factory or foundry in Moorfield, purchased by Wesley in 1739 and established as the first center of Methodist witness and work in London. Nelson F. Adams' "Musical Sources for John Wesley's Tune books: the Genealogy of 148 Tunes" identifies the sources for the collection's forty-two tunes as follows: German, fifteen; English, twenty-two; secular adaptation, one; original to the collection, four. Adams also provides important commentary on each tune (Adams 1973, 70).

The significance of the *Collection's* subtitle "Set to Music, As They are commonly sung at the Foundery" is not clear, although it is probable that Wesley taught tunes by rote to the society, particularly those melodies he adapted as settings for his brother's texts, written in greatly expanded meters. The 1742 collection served as the tunebook for *Hymns and Sacred Poems,* 1739, 1740, and 1742. The tunes, most of which are printed in sequence by meter, are cross-referenced to the page number in the appropriate collection designated volume 1, 2, or 3.

Beginning with Lightwood's "Notes on the Foundery Tune-Book," 1900, commentators have cited the *Collection's* errors, much of it faulty copying of tunes from primary and secondary sources, causing incorrect key signatures, measure barring, melodic lines, and the misplacements of syllabic accents. Mistakes in notation also resulted from Wesley's adaptations of tunes to accommodate the particular meter of a text, including those by his brother Charles, and John's faulty memory of the tunes for which he apparently had no printed source.

One of the most profound copying errors is the tune JERICHO, adapted from the first violin part in Handel's opera *Riccardo Primo,* 1727, and printed above the treble clef. After the gross musical errors have been cited and accounted for, the task remains to explain the accurate transcriptions, e.g., SAVANNAH from Freylinghausen's *Geistreiches Gesangbuch,* 1704 (Wesley's annotated copy is in the Wesleyan archives in Manchester), and LONDON NEW TUNE from Playford's *Divine Companion,* 1701. The only plausible conclusion is that Wesley had the services of a competent music editor. Some scholars, including O. A. Beckerlegge (Wesley 1983, 738), have suggested that it was Thomas Butts whom Wesley employed as the Foundery's bookkeeper from 1742 to 1753 and who compiled *Harmonia Sacra,* ca. 1756. The musically flawed 1742 collection apparently prompted Wesley's engagement of an unnamed editor or editors to assist in the preparation of the 1761 and 1780 collections.

The *Foundery Collection* was the testing ground for Wesley's view that congregational song was important in linking Methodism's characteristic preaching services, society meetings, love feasts, and annual meetings. Guiding his selection of the tunes were the breadth of the societies' tastes and varying levels of musical instruction. Nelson F. Adams' description of each genre (Adams 1973, 64-66) and his careful annotations of the lineage of the 148 tunes in the 1742, 1761, and 1780 *Collections* (Adams 1973, 73-197) provide invaluable insight into Wesley's impressive ability to select from the repertory of eighteenth-century tune collections.

John Wesley's first tune collection, in spite of its error-filled music, shows his sure instinct to select solid tunes in a variety of meters as evidenced by these tunes that are still included in Methodist and other hymnals. The bold face numbers indicate the pages in *The United Methodist Hymnal,* 1989.

AMSTERDAM (76.76.77.76), **96**
CAREY'S (SURREY) (88.88.88), **579**

EASTER HYMN (77.77D), **302**
HANOVER (10.10.11), **181**
OLD 113TH (888.888), **60**
SAVANNAH (77.77), **385**
TALLIS' CANON (LM), **682**
UFFINGHAM (LM), **450**
VATER UNSER (88.88.88), **414**
WER NUR DEN LIEBEN GOTT (98.98.88), **142**

## The Singing Tradition of Early Methodists

Methodist singing practice evolved from two traditions: late seventeenth-century Anglican parish psalm singing, the "old way of singing," and the Moravians' spirited *Singstunde* (singing hour).

The "old way of singing," had prompted this scornful verse from John Wilmot, 1647-80, Earl of Rochester:

> Sternhold and Hopkins had great qualms
> When they translated David's psalms,
>   To make the heart right glad;
> But had it been King David's fate
> To hear thee sing and them translate
>   By God! 'twould set him mad!
>             (Reynolds and Price 1987, 37)

Nicholas Temperley has commented on the popularity of seventeenth-century Anglican parish psalm singing among common folk in country churches:

> "The old way of singing," together with the lining out that went with it, was unacceptable or laughable to educated people of the time [late seventeenth and early eighteenth century] as it probably would be to us today. . . . The reformers could get rid of the old way, but could not easily replace it with a musical tradition which the people would feel to be theirs. Not until the

Methodists brought a second wave of folk tunes into the churches would genuinely congregational singing be heard again (Temperley 1979, 99).

"Old singing style" tempos were apparently very slow, and the melodies lacked the rhythm of the chorale or Genevan psalter tunes. Nicholas Temperley cites Thomas Mathew's discussion of tempo in his 1688 psalm book:

> He said that three notes were in use in psalm tunes, the breve, semibreve and minim; he defined their duration as either, four and two 'pulses at the wrist of a person in good health and temper.'. . . The singing was also interrupted by the lining out between phrases. Any sense of the tune as a whole, and as originally conceived, must have been almost completely lost (Temperley 1979, 93).

Temperley comments that the duration of the whole note would be a little over two seconds and that the slow tempo allowed individual singers to improvise embellishments between the notes. "Additional notes were often inserted, making a kind of ornamentation" (Temperley 1979, 93).

Wesley in "Reasons against a Separation," 1758, described this as singing in a "slow drawling manner" (see page 65). Wesley also apparently includes his objections to this practice in his "Directions for Singing":

> V. Sing *modestly*. Do not baul [bawl], so as to be heard above, or distinct from the rest of the congregation, that you may not destroy the harmony; but strive to unite your voices together, so as to make one clear melodious sound.
>
> VI. Sing in *Time*: whatever time is sung be sure to keep with it. Do not run before nor stay behind it; but attend close to the leading voice, and move therewith as exactly as you can; and take care you sing not *too slow*. This drawling way naturally steals on all who are lazy; and it is

high time to drive it out from among us, and sing all our
tunes just as quick as we did at first.

The "old style" tune repertory was in three meters: common meter
(CM), 86.86, that was adapted from the Old English ballad meter known
as "fourteener"; short meter (SM), 86.86, a variant of common meter,
and long meter, 88.88, a favorite meter of the Latin office hymn.
Familiar tunes could be sung to a number of texts in the same meter;
which resulted in the use of relatively few tunes. There was probably little consideration of a tune as complimenting the meaning and spirit of
a given text.

The role of the leader of congregational song was basically to select
the tune, set the pitch, line out the text sometimes only a few words at a
time, start the phrase, wait for it to finish, then line out another.

It is clear that this type of singing is extremely conservative in nature. Deliberate innovations were not part
of the old way of singing, for no self-conscious or creative musicians were involved in it. New tunes were
neither wanted nor expected (Temperley 1979, 97).

### Moravian-Style Singing

The second influence on early Methodist singing practice was the
Moravians. Eighteenth-century Moravian-style congregational song,
formed in part from the traditions of the fifteenth-century Hussite
*Unitas fratrum* (Bohemian Brethren), "had its own individual stamp
through the [*Singstunde* (singing hour) that Count Zinzendorf, 1700-60,
see page 158] introduced in Herrnhut and other localities, probably
fashioned after the Halle practices under [August H.] Francke" (Blume
1974, 600). Walter Blankenburg comments on Zinzendorf's views on
music:

Some of Zinzendorf's remarks suggest that singing and
the hours of song were to him the focal points of spiritual and congregational life. He felt that there were
ways to a genuine expression of enthusiastic pietistic

faith and therefore a measure of the spiritual condition of the congregation. He said of the songs that they were "the best method to bring God's truth to the heart and to preserve it there. . . . At the hours of song, which took place daily for many years, there was, frequently for homiletic reasons, improvised singing carried out by combining verses, even half verses, chosen at random sometimes even on spontaneously invented new texts. Complete songs were customarily sung only at the Sunday sermon services (Blume 1974, 600-01).

The Moravians, following Lutheran pietistic practice, used choirs, organs, and other instruments in worship. John Wesley was deeply moved by their *Singstunde*, singing meeting or singing hour (see pages 34), as well as their hymns and tunes from Freylinghausen's collections, which entered the mainstream of English evangelical song through the Wesleys. See "John Wesley's 1737 Charlestown *Collection of Psalms and Hymns*," pages 34-56.

Early Methodist singing practice is described by James T. Lightwood:

The hearty character of Methodist singing at the Foundery and other meeting-houses soon attracted notice. Included in the various references to it in current literature is an interesting statement by Dr. John Scott in his *Fine Picture of Enthusiasm*, 1744. He acknowledges that the Methodists have got some of the most melodious tunes that ever were composed for church music. 'There is great harmony in their singing, and it is very enchanting' (Lightwood 1927, 24).

Methodists had in common with other evangelical groups the performance practice of singing alternately in groups, usually men and women, sometimes using the form of the dialogue hymn, a distinct contribution of John Cennick (Lightwood 1905, 144). Women usually sat in separate sections of Methodist chapels, and in part-songs their part was probably not doubled by men, as noted in answer 9 to question 39 in the "Large" *Minutes:*

> (9) Let the women constantly sing their parts alone. Let no man sing with them, unless he understands the notes, and sings the bass, as it is pricked down in the book.

James T. Lightwood comments that the number of hymns used in early Methodist worship was limited to two only, one before and one after the sermon. Such was the rule at the Foundery, and for some time it seems to have prevailed everywhere. There were times, however, when the singing of a hymn proved a serviceable antidote to certain disturbances organized by opponents of the Methodist preachers [see excerpts from Charles Wesley's *Journal,* pages 118-52] (Lightwood 1927, 34).

Lightwood continues with comment on the practice of singing psalms:

> The custom of sitting during the singing of the Psalms prevailed largely in the churches, but it did not find favour amongst the Methodists. When Wesley was at Kendal in 1753 he found that the people kept their seats during the singing of the first hymn, nor did they attempt to join in, 'though they knew the tune, but after the sermon they joined in.' Shortly after, when preaching at Sligo, he noticed that 'scarce any one either sung or stood at the Psalms, so that I was almost alone therein. But in the afternoon almost every one stood up, and most of them sung or endeavoured to do so' [June 29, 1760] (Lightwood 1927, 35).

In 1788 Wesley writes to quell a controversy in Millbourn Place, stemming in part from the question of chanting the psalms: "My objection to the chanting the psalms was, we have no such thing among the Methodists" (*Proceedings* 1904, 4:228).

The number of hymns sung in preaching services, the love feast, watchnight, and covenant services apparently varied with the occasion, the presence of trained musicians, and the ability of the group to recall old favorites and learn new hymns. Controversy continued late in Wesley's ministry concerning the number of hymns to be sung in the service, where they would be placed in the order of the service, and to what tunes they would be sung. One instance of this dispute in Norwich has been traced by James Redfearn in the exchange of letters between Wesley, superintendent Thomas Wride, and local preachers John Muckarsay and James M. Byron. On December 14, 1785, Wesley wrote Muchersey [*sic.*] and Byron:

> If you do not chuse to obey me, you need not: I will let you go when you please & send other Preachers in your place. If you do chuse to stay with me, never sing more than twice; Once before & once after Sermon (*Proceedings* 1897, 1:143).

On December 30 Wride replied:

> If the person who succeeds me be not particularly fitted he will have an uneasy time of it. He should know the Methodist tunes & be resolved to Sing them only. . . . It would be well that he should know a little of Musick or else their little knowledge will give them great advantage over him. . . . Brother Muckarsay [has continued] keeping to his three time singing [and] has set them [the society] on their high Horse. . . . Since your letter to B. Muckarsay & Byron the three times singing is over. But, it has made the Heys outrageous with me. Brother Byron says he has not given out more than twice at one Service, since he knew that it was disagreeable unto you: But that once since; the Heys burst out with what they pleased without him, but to prevent them for the future, He Prays before the Singing (*Proceedings* 1897, 1:144).

James Redfearn provides these further comments:

> Notwithstanding the desire of Wesley and many of the
> earlier preachers, the practice of singing more elaborate
> music, and more frequently than twice in the services,
> gradually became general, whilst select bands and early
> morning preaching fell into desuetude. During the tran-
> sition stage fierce disputes arose between the adherents
> of the old and new schools. In the case at Norwich,
> indeed, the conflict became so sharp that Wride was
> locked out of the chapel by the infuriated singers and
> others, and had perforce to preach in the street
> (*Proceedings* 1897, 1:145).

J. C. C. Probert comments on the variety of singing practices in
Cornwall during Wesley's time:

> At Hugas an old man who sat in the square leaders' seat
> [in the front of the chapel] pitched the tune, and the
> hymns were sung 2 lines at a time. At Penryn W. in the
> early days a leader pitched the tune often with a penny
> whistle, and the hymns were sung two lines at a time.
> If the leader was absent it was not uncommon for some
> to sing a common metre and some a long. At
> Mousehole W. the precentor used a tuning fork. Hymns
> were usually lined out for two reasons: the inability of
> most to read the words and the shortage of hymn books
> (Probert 1978, 50).

This practice of giving out the hymn, whereby the leader sang two
lines of a hymn followed by the congregation repeating the same two
lines, was the standard way to sing familiar hymns as well as teach new
hymns and tunes. As lead singers, choirs and organs joined to  support
the singing, a new practice evolved, whereby everyone read a stanza,
the choir sang that stanza, followed by the congregation and choir
singing together. Given the time needed to sing an entire hymn either in
two-line or whole verse fashion, it is little wonder why relatively few
hymns were sung. See Wesley's exchange with Thomas Wride, page 61.

The new practice became a source of conflict between musician and minister. James T. Lightwood comments, "The singers did not like it [the old way], though it is evident that the ministers did" (Lightwood 1928, 52). After nearly a half-century of controversy the 1844 Conference decided the matter in this resolution:

> Mode of Giving out Hymns. Complaints having been made that, in some of our chapels, the novel practice has been introduced of reading and singing a whole verse of a hymn at once, instead of our usual and regular plan of giving out successive portions of verses, the Conference hereby records its serious disapproval of this innovation, as being inconvenient and injurious, especially to the poorer classes of our fellow-worshippers, and not generally conducive to edification (Lightwood 1928, 51).

The four worship and singing spaces most mentioned by John and Charles in their journals and letters are the Foundery, Wesley's Chapel in London, Kingswood School near Bath, and the New Room in Bristol— each with unique seating arrangements and acoustics and presumably different performance practices. Only Wesley's Chapel and the New Room are still standing.

By mid-century Methodists were widely heralded as a singing people. Oliver A. Beckerlegge has commented that throughout England,

> Methodists everywhere became well known for their singing. The Cornish Methodists, for example, were nicknamed 'the Canorum', from a Cornish word canor, which means 'a singer'. In Yorkshire, John Pawson went to Otley to hear the Methodists. He listened to 'an excellent sermon', was impressed by the devout behaviour of the congregation, and 'was highly delighted with the singing'. As a young man Thomas Olivers left with most of the congregation when public preaching ended, because society meetings were for members only, but he 'used to go into the field at the back of the preaching-house, and listen while they sang the praises of God (Wesley 1983, 62).

A visitor, Joseph Williams of Kidderminster, commented in his journal for Tuesday, September 18, 1739:

> He [Charles Wesley] concluded with Singing, Prayer, & the usual Benediction. . . . Before he would take any bodily Refreshment he with a few friends that waited on him, sung an Hymn & then prayed for a Blessing . . . After the Tea we sung another Hymn. I could not fall in with their way of singing in the Field, for they sung German Tunes, keeping very quick time; but in the House, after a stanza or two, I fell in readily enough, & with great Elevation of Soul (Leaver 1994, 3).

Thomas Vivian, Curate of Redruth, Cornwall, in 1747 commented on Methodist hymn singing.

> In publick prayer I hear they frequently shed tears, especially in singing their hymns. [Their societies] meet every Wednesday and Sunday evening to pray and sing hymns and psalms. [In the classes they] meet together to sing and pray with their leader once or twice a week (Probert 1978, 3-4).

Johan Henrik Liden, a professor at the University of Upsala, visited the Foundery on Sunday, Oct. 15, 1769, and made these comments in his *Journal* about Methodists' hymn singing:

> The song of the Methodists is the most beautiful I ever heard. Their fine psalms have exceedingly beautiful melodies composed by great masters. They sing in a proper way, with devotion, serene mind and charm. It added not a little to the harmonious charm of the song that some lines were sung only by the women and afterwards the whole congregation joined in the Chorus (*Proceedings* 1929, 17:3).

In 1757 John Wesley boasted of the singing practices of Methodists compared with those of the established church:

[Methodists'] solemn addresses to God [are not] interrupted either by the formal drawl of a parish clerk, the
screaming of boys, who bawl out what they neither feel
nor understand, or the unreasonable and unmeaning
impatience of a voluntary on the organ. When it is sea-
sonable to sing praise to God, they do it with the spirit,
and with the understanding also; not in the miserable,
scandalous doggerel of Hopkins and Sternhold, but in
psalms and hymns which are both sense and poetry;
such as would sooner provoke a critic to turn Christian,
than a Christian to turn critic. What they sing is therefore a proper continuation of the spiritual and reason-
able service; being selected for that end (not by a poor
humdrum wretch who can scarce read what he drones
out with an air of importance, but) by one who knows
what he is about, and how to connect the preaching with
the following part of the service. Nor does he take just
'two staves', but more or less, as may best raise the soul
to God; especially when sung in well-composed and
well-adapted tunes, not by a handful of wild, unawak-
ened striplings, but by a whole serious congregation;
and these, not lolling at ease, or in the indecent posture
of sitting, drawling out one word after another, but all
standing before God, and praise him lustily and with a
good courage (Wesley 1984, 13:217).

Wesley warns his preachers in "Reasons against a Separation," 1758,
that they should not imitate the dissenters in praying and singing.
Concerning the latter he comments:

One might add, neither should we sing, like them, in a
slow drawling manner—we sing swift, both because it
saves time, and because it tends to awake and enliven
the soul (Wesley 1989, 9:340).

Wesley comments following a visit with Methodists on the Isle of
Man:

[June 6, 1781] . . . the preaching house contained all that could come. Afterwards, Mr. Crook desired me to meet the singers. I was agreeably surprised. I have not heard better singing either at Bristol or London. Many, both men and women, have admirable voices; and they sing with good judgment. Who would have expected this in the Isle of Man? (Wesley 1872, 4:206).

### Other Tune Books Used by Methodists

The *Foundery Collection* was apparently never reprinted; the societies perhaps found it had limited value and turned instead to existing collections, possibly including George Whitefield's tune collection *Divine Musical Miscellany*, "being A Collection of Psalm, and Hymn Tunes, 1754," the tune book for his *Collection of Hymns for Social Worship*, 1753, prepared for his rival congregation in his Tabernacle near the Foundery. Maurice Frost suggests that Whitefield and Butts (*Harmonia Sacra*, ca. 1756) used a common stock they applied in the two distinct collections. While twenty-two of the twenty-four tunes in John F. Lampe's *Hymns on the Great Festivals and Other Occasions*, 1746, are included in Butts, only RESURRECTION was included in Whitefield's tune book. The collection's music editor is unknown, but its subtitle, "great part of which were never before in Print," suggests the work of one of many knowledgeable musicians in the evangelical movement, including the Wesleys' friend and colleague, John Cennick, who for a time directed the singing classes at the Tabernacle.

Butts may have used the failure of the 1742 collection as a compelling reason for compiling *Harmonia Sacra*, 1756. While 1756 is the earliest probable date for the collection, Nicholas Temperley has found advertisements for its sale that appeared in 1754 (November 1993 correspondence with Carlton R. Young).

Butts presumably prepared his collection for Methodist societies, groups the Wesleys were beginning to divide into smaller classes. This development greatly increased the market for suitable tune books, including his collection and others published from 1750 to 1770.

Lightwood comments that these collections seem to have been designed to attract the attention of the Methodist leaders of singing.

> One industrious psalmodist, Thomas Knibb, published several tune-books [*The Psalm Singers Help*, ca. 1765; *The Psalm Singers Help, A New Edition*, ca. 1775]. . . . [The former] "contained a special supplement with the heading "The tunes from page 96 to the end of the book, being used by Methodists, are suited to their metres" (Lightwood 1927, 24).

Another collection apparently prepared for Methodists is the twenty-two tunes appended to *A Collection of Hymns and Sacred Poems,* 1749, printed in Dublin by S. Powell. Some, including Lightwood, have suggested that since John Wesley and John F. Lampe were in Ireland in 1749, the former may have been the compiler and the latter the music editor. Frank Baker, however, states that there "is not the the slightest likelihood of their collaborating" (Correspondence with Carlton R. Young, July 1994). John Wesley's involvement is possibly hinted, but should not be presumed, in the inclusion in the preface of Charles Wesley's hymn "O thou God of harmony and love" (1747), probably composed to mark the conversion of Lampe. (See pages 178-80 for the text with commentary.) One interlined stanza is included in the *Collection's* supplement. Further, while a great number of the 295 hymns in the collection are by Isaac Watts, many Charles Wesley hymns are included, e.g., "Hail the day that sees him rise" and "Rejoice, the Lord is King" as well as John Wesley's translations from the German, "Lo, God is here, let us adore" and from the French "World adieu, thou real cheat." Hymns from *Hymns on the Lord's Supper*, 1745, are found in the sections on Holy Communion and Baptism.

The *Collection's* supplement of twenty-two tunes includes eight German and English tunes that appear in the *Foundery Collection,* 1742. SALISBURY TUNE, in the 1742 *Collection* set to Charles Wesley's "Christ the Lord, is risen today," is here set to his "Hark, how all the welkin rings." Other standard tunes such as ST. ANNE are included as well as new tunes, for example the apparent folk-derived IRISH. The music, in contrast to the 1742 *Collection* (see pages 54-56), is well edited, clearly set, and printed, reflecting the work of a skilled editor—probably not Lampe, but as Frank Baker suggests it could have been John Cennick, who occasionally used Powell to print his works (Correspondence with Carlton R. Young, July 1994). Lampe however, would probably have included more tunes from *Hymns for the Great Festivals,* 1746, than INVITATION that is transposed up one step to F major and printed without a figured bass. Here, as in the 1746 collection, this tune is set with Charles Wesley's text "Sinners obey the Gospel word."

The only extant copy of this volume is in the Warrington Collection at Clifford E. Barbour Library, Pittsburgh Theological Seminary, Pittsburgh, Pennsylvania. A copy of the *Collection* was obtained, courtesy of John J. Fry, Public Services Librarian. So far as this writer can ascertain, the music sources of the supplement have not been determined except for Nelson F. Adams' tracing eight tunes to the *Foundery Collection* (Adams 1973, 273-354).

### *Select Hymns with Tunes Annext,: John Wesley's Second Tune Book*

Wesley's next collection was *Select Hymns with Tunes Annext,: Designed chiefly for the USE of the People Called Methodists,* 1761, usually referred to as *Sacred Melody.* There were 122 tunes in the first edition, and twelve were added in later printings. The tunes were arranged by meter beginning with short meter (66. 8. 6). His preface to this collection (Wesley 1761, iii) is of inestimable value in understanding his authority and influence in shaping the music of the revival. It begins with Wesley's praise for Butts's collection.

> 1. Some years ago a Collection of Tunes was published, under the title of *Harmonia Sacra.* I believe all unprejudiced persons who understand music allow, that it exceeds beyond all degrees of comparison, any thing of the kind which has appeared in England before.

Butts was an employee in the Foundery from 1742 to 1753, and may have helped prepare the flawed *Foundery Collection,* which may in part explain Wesley's lavish praise. It is also likely that Wesley assisted Butts in the selection of the tunes as well as the texts, particularly those of Charles Wesley. The preface continues: "The tunes being admirably well chosen."

The ninety-two tunes in Butts's collection are from twenty-nine sources, including eighteen from the *Foundery Collection* and twenty-two of the twenty-four tunes from John F. Lampe's *Hymns on the Great Festivals and Other Occasions*, 1746 (Frost 1952, 69-70). Butts included Lampe's tunes in their original two-part settings and also in three voices with a soprano part set above the tune.

In describing the collection as "accurately engraven," Wesley may be alluding to the 1742 collection's flawed editing and copying. In pointing out that Butts's collection is scored "not only for the voice, but likewise for the orgain [*sic.*] or harpsichord," Wesley appears to be defending the unison-unaccompanied format of both his 1742 and his 1761 collections, contrasted with a number of contemporary collections scored for two or three voices, organ or harpsichord, and figured bass (in evangelical chapels, a cello [viol] sometimes doubled the bass line). His views on the primacy of unison singing are set forth in "Thoughts on the Power of Music." For Wesley's text and this writer's commentary see pages 84-93.

In the next paragraph Wesley articulates his assumed role as custodian of the Methodist societies' tune repertory and arbiter of the performance practice, a role beginning with the publication of the failed *Foundery Collection* and extending through Butts's successful collection, which continued to be sold in the Foundery after the publication of *Sacred Melody*.

> 2. But this, tho' it is excellent in its kind, is not the thing which I want. I want the people called *Methodists* to sing true, the tunes which are in *common use* among them.

While it is not clear what constitutes "the tunes which are in common use" in the societies, 92 tunes from *Harmonia Sacra* comprise the

102 tunes in *Sacred Melody* (Frost 1952, 78). It is worth noting that rival George Whitefield's tune collection, *Divine Musical Miscellany*, 1754, may have also been used by some societies. If, as Maurice Frost suggests, *Harmonia Sacra* and *Divine Musical Miscellany* were derived from the same sources, one can imply that Wesley's comments may also be directed towards Whitefield's collection.

In the next sentence Wesley establishes his paradigm of evangelical hymnic publishing: focused content, modest size, and low cost.

> At the same time I want them to have in one volume, the *best Hymns* which we have printed: and that in a *small* and *portable* volume, and one of an *easy price*.

Wesley's two-decade rift with musicians and music editors apparently began with the production of the faulted *Foundery Collection*, and his view is expressed in the next paragraph. While it is unknown whom Wesley deemed an acceptable and amiable music editor, it might have been Thomas Butts who probably "collaborated with Wesley in the production of [the collection's] *Gamut*" (Wesley 1983, 739).

> 3. I have been endeavouring for more than 20 years to procure such a book as this. But in vain: Masters of music were above following any direction but their own. And I was determined whoever compiled this, should follow *my* direction: Not *mending* our tunes, but setting them down, neither better nor worse than they were. At length I have prevailed.

The preface closes with Wesley's summary of the content and purpose of this combination text and tune collection:

> The following collection contains all the tunes which are in common use among us. They are pricked true, exactly as I desire all our congregation may sing them: and here is prefix to them a collection of those hymns which are (I think) some of the best we have published.

The volume likewise is small, as well as the price. This therefore I recommend preferable to all others.

Wesley's tune-only format may be considered a rejection of part-singing and other performance considerations such as figured bass and excessive ornaments. Wesley excluded the tunes adapted from G. F. Handel's and other composers' operas that Butts included in his collection. As for choir music Wesley placed one anthem-tune, CHESHUNT, at the end of the 1770 edition of *Sacred Melody* and included five others in the 1788 edition of *Sacred Harmony:* THE 100 PSALM, SPRING, THE DYING CHRISTIAN, DENBIGH, and YARMOUTH. Wesley had apparently been forced to include them because of the popularity of the village singing groups and their influence on the singing practice of local Methodist societies.

A group of parishioners would meet together, perhaps in the vestry or outside the church altogether, to learn the principles of music notation from a traveling teacher or from the parish clerk, and to rehearse psalm tunes in harmony. . . . When once the choirs were established, they wanted to sing more ambitious music than old psalm tunes, and in this they were encouraged by some disinterested musicians and a few clergymen, and exploited by enterprising music publishers and singing teachers (Temperley 1979, 152, 202).

For comment on late nineteenth-century Anglican parish music and its influence on Methodist music see "Urban parish church music" and "Country psalmody" in Nicholas Temperley's *Music of the English Parish Church*, Vol. 1. See also page 79.

The success of *Harmonia Sacra* was apparently not obscured by the publication of *Sacred Melody* since, as Beckerlegge notes, it continued to be sold at the Foundery as late as 1777 (Wesley 1983, 739), and it continued to form the core of *Sacred Harmony*, 1780.

### Wesley's Directions for Singing

Wesley's attempts to standardize hymn singing performance practice and repertory are seen in his seven directions for singing which he included following the tunes index in *Select Hymns with Tunes Annext: Designed chiefly for the USE of the People Called Methodists*, 1761, ed. 1770.

*That this part of Divine Worship may be the more acceptable to God, as well as the more profitable to yourself and others, be careful to observe the following directions.*

I. LEARN *these* Tunes before you learn any others; afterwards learn as many as you please.

II. Sing them exactly as they are printed here, without altering or mending them at all; and if you have learned to sing them otherwise, unlearn it as soon as you can.

III. Sing *All*. See that you join with the congregation as frequently as you can. Let not a slight degree of weakness or weariness hinder you. If it is a cross to you, take it up and you will find a blessing.

IV. Sing *lustily* and with good courage. Beware of singing as if you were half dead, or half asleep; but lift up your voice with strength. Be no more afraid of your voice now, nor more ashamed of its being heard, than when you sung the songs of *Satan*.

V. Sing *modestly*. Do not baul [bawl], so as to be heard a-above, or distinct from the rest of the congregation, that you may not destroy the harmony; but strive to unite your voices together, so as to make one clear melodious sound.

VI. Sing in *Time*: whatever time is sung be sure to keep with it. Do not run before nor stay behind it; but attend close to the leading voice, and move therewith as exactly as you can; and take care you sing not *too slow*. This drawling way naturally steals on all who are lazy; and it is high time to drive it out from among us, and sing all our tunes just as quick as we did at first.

VII. Above all sing *spiritually*. Have an eye to God in every word you sing. Aim at pleasing Him more than yourself, or any other creature. In order to [do] this attend strictly to the sense of what you sing, and see that your *Heart* is not carried away with the sound, but offered to God continually; so shall your singing be such as the *Lord* will approve of here, and reward [you] when he cometh in the clouds of heaven.

The directions can be  summarized as follows:

    1. Learn these tunes
    2. Sing them exactly
    3. Sing all
    4. Sing lustily
    5. Sing modestly
    6. Sing in time
    7. Sing spiritually.

S T Kimbrough, Jr., has commented on Wesley's directions:

Why were these [seven] major points in the Directions made at this time? (1761)? Why these seven? What is cardinal about them? . . . I suspect that part of what is behind the directions is that with a core of good tunes in prevalent meters one could sing many different hymns. . . . For example, in *Select Hymns*, 1761, most tunes are assigned to more than one hymn. Above all, I think the Wesleys had come to understand the power of the wedding of text and tune as the most vital way of celebrating and remembering faith, scripture, theology, and the task of social service. The hymns had become the "theological memory" of the Methodist movement, and if the singing of them were imprecise and nonchalant, so would be the theology of the church. One could perhaps find directions 1-6 in any good book on hymn or choral singing, but No. 7 is the crowning direction of John Wesley and the Methodist movement (Correspondence with Carlton R. Young, June 1992).

The Directions parallel concerns about singing that Wesley had included in his "Large" *Minutes* (see pages 94-95) as questions and answers distilled from decades of wide-ranging conversations with Methodist preachers. Wesley's lifelong efforts to standardize the rhetoric and music of congregational song—the unity of emotion and the cognate, the heart and the head—became a distinctive mark of the eighteenth-century Methodist revival in Britain.

While the directions in *Sacred Melody* were addressed to a general audience, Wesley on at least one occasion compiled a set of rules for local use for the forty-three singers in the Dublin society. A copy of a page of the rules is included in plate 108, page 62, *The Oxford Companion to Music*, 1970 ed.

1. The persons who at present learn to sing . . . . [43 names in three columns follow].
2. Let these meet at the New Room every Thursday evening.
3. Let them, and them only, sit on the second and third seats of the gallery on each side of the pulpit.
4. Let an account be kept of all who are absent from the Singing Meeting on Thursday evening, or the Singing Fest on Sunday.

Wesley, probably assisted by Thomas Butts, also prepared "The Gamut, or Scale of Music," a twelve-page short course in note reading and music theory that was placed before the tunes. According to O. A. Beckerlegge, Wesley's "Gamut," while similar in intent, is not based on any of the introductions included in the vast number of mid- and late-eighteenth-century tune books. Wesley's customizing of the introduction is consistent with his intent for the collection to serve the special needs of the "People called Methodist." O. A. Beckerlegge has commened:

> While Wesley's own *Gamut* (for which no prototype has
> been discovered) reads rather strangely to modern ears,
> and whilst some of his terminology is now outdated, it
> must be said that it is far easier to follow than those of
> most of his contemporaries. . . . The difference is that
> while Wesley's could be read by the unskilled on his
> own (for the most part), [others] required the personal
> explanation of a music master (Wesley 1983, 739).

The "Gamut" was included until 1765 when Wesley substituted "The
Grounds of Vocal Music" (Wesley 1983, 752). The present writer's
research is based on "The Grounds of Vocal Music," included in *Select
Hymns with Tunes Annext,* Third Edition, Corrected and Enlarged, 1770.
The tunes are preceded with a title page: *Sacred Melody or Choice
Collection of Psalm and Hymn Tunes with a Short Introduction.*

In the "Grounds" Wesley simplified the technical language and
reduced the number of musical illustrations, e.g., the paragraph on the
trill in the 1761 edition:

> There are several Graces in Music, but the most princi-
> ple is a Trill; which is the Shaking of two distinct Notes
> easily upon one Syllable, as long as the Time allows,
> always beginning with the upper, thus [here was includ-
> ed a notated example] it ought to be used on all descend-
> ing Prick'd Crotchets; and always before a Close; also
> on all descending sharp'd Notes; and on all descending
> Semitones; but none shorter than Crotchets (Wesley
> 1761, viii).

In the third edition, 1770, this is reduced:

> A tril [*sic.*] is the shaking of two distinct Notes easily
> upon one Syllable as long as the Time allows and is
> marked thus *tr.* (Wesley 1770, vi).

A portion of the revised "Gamut" is a carefully designed do-it-your-
self method of note learning. For example, the music editor succinctly

describes in simple terms the notes and their placement on the lines and spaces of the treble clef:

> II. The *Notes* in Music are usually placed within five Lines. If there be an extraordinary Line above or below these, it is termed a *Ledger Line*.
>
> There are in all *seven Notes* and no more, represented by the seven first Letters of the Alphabet. There seem indeed to be more in most Tunes: but they are only a repetition of these. In writing them C is placed on a ledger Line below, D on the Space below the first Line, reckoning upwards, E on the first Line, F on the first Space, G on the second Line, A on the second Space, B on the third line, C on the third Space. This is called an *Octave*, being the Eighth Note from the former C.

Then follow a number of not-so-simple descriptions and illustrations of intervals, tempo markings, called moods, e.g.:

> In *Adagio* a Semibreve takes up the time wherein a Pendulum strikes four strokes: in *Largo* the time wherein it strikes three strokes. In *Allegro* the time wherein it strikes two strokes.

It is worth noting that these and other tempo markings are apparently not used in this collection, although they are included in *Sacred Harmony*. Their inclusion in *Sacred Melody* supports the view that this section may have been adapted by Wesley or his music editor from another set of instructions in another collection.

Time signatures are surveyed and defined; for example,

> *Triple Time* is marked either thus 3/2, and then three Minnums (Two of which are equal to a Semibreve) are contained in A Bar.

The directions for leading congregational song are very explicit:

To *Beat Time*, in slow Common Time, at the first stroke of the Pendulum strike your hand down; at the second move it to the Right, at the third lift it up, at the fourth move it to the Left. Or (which is more common) sing the first two Notes, (Or first half) of the Bar, with the hand down, and the last half with it up.

In beating *Triple Time*, the first two-thirds of the Bar are usually sung with the hand down; and the last third part of it with the hand up: always observing that the hand must be put down, at the beginning of every perfect Bar; both in Common and Triple Time.

Clefs, note and rest values, and repeat signs are defined and illustrated. This section closes with a method of transposition that makes it possible to contain all tunes within the clef.

In the 1765 revision, Wesley substituted for the "Gamut" seven "Lessons for exercising the Voice," three pages of intervalic exercises. Wesley concludes the lessons with this admonition:

Let each of these Lessons be got off perfectly and by heart in the Order they are here placed, so that they all may be sung readily and exactly both in Time and Tune.

The lessons, as well as the method of transposition, use the prevailing round-note four-syllabic system of solmization, whereby the diatonic major scale is sung fa, sol, la, fa, sol, la, mi, fa. The half-steps are between the third and fourth steps of the scale—fa and sol—and the seventh and eighth—mi and fa. The following illustrates solmization in the key of C:

Fa  Sol  La  Fa  Sol  La  Mi  Fa
C    D    E   F    G    A    B    C

This method of sight-reading was used by USA eighteenth-century compilers John Tufts and Thomas Walter. In the early nineteenth century this approach was also used with slight variations by William Smith, William Little, and Andrew Law.

> Smith and Little used a right-angle triangle for *fa*; a circle, or round head, for *sol*; a square for *la*; and a diamond head for *mi*—all on the five-line music staff. Law used the same four shapes with slightly different arrangement. His *fa* was square, his *la* was the right-angle triangle, and he eliminated the use of the staff. It was the Smith and Little pattern of the shape of the noteheads that was used extensively in the Southern [oblong] folk hymn publications (Reynolds and Price 1987, 88).

*Sacred Melody* is John Wesley's most creative, complete, and characteristically Methodist approach to compiling congregational song. The 1765 edition's revised "Gamut" met the emerging need for indigenous music leaders, if they are to be effective, to have technical, theoretical, and practical skills. It was this collection to which Wesley constantly refers to as "our tune-book" and "our tunes"; for example, answers 12 and 8 to question 39 in the "Large" *Minutes:*

> (12) Recommend our tune-book everywhere; and if you cannot sing yourself choose a person or two in each place to pitch the tune for you.

> (8) In every large society let them learn to sing; and let them always learn our own tunes first.

Here Wesley appears to begin an accommodation in his repertory to the growing influence of choirs in parish and Methodist worship.

### Sacred Harmony: John Wesley's Third Tune Book

Wesley's final tune book is *Sacred Harmony, or A choice Collection of Psalm and Hymn Tunes In two or three parts for the Voice, harpsichord & Organ,* 1780. There are 104 tunes arranged according to meter, 31 meters in all (Wesley 1983, 772), most of them harmonized versions of tunes in *Sacred Melody*. In 1786 *Sacred Harmony* became the first Methodist tune collection to serve one hymnal when, beginning with the fifth edition of his 1780 *Collection,* Wesley put a tune name from *Sacred Harmony* over each text. James T. Lightwood comments:

> Wesley evidently approved of the 'fixed tune' system, and would doubtless feel he had done all he could to prevent irresponsible leaders of the singing from introducing new tunes composed by themselves or their friends (Lightwood 1928, 8).

As with the previous collection, *Sacred Harmony* was broad in sources and styles, and according to Oliver A. Beckerlegge some tunes "must have been composed by local amateur musicians whose tunes Wesley had heard in some local society, and to which he took a fancy. . . . [Nevertheless] the vast majority had already been chosen by Wesley from Butts's *Harmonia Sacra"* (Wesley 1983, 771), and had already been included in *Sacred Melody*, 1761.

Oliver A. Beckerlegge and Frank Baker have annotated each tune in the collection in Wesley 1983, 772-87. See also pages 120-97 in Nelson F. Adams, "The Musical Sources for John Wesley's Tune-Books: the Genealogy of 148 Tunes," for sources and additional commentary about the tunes in *Sacred Melody* and *Sacred Harmony*.

Wesley's final tune collection marks several important accommodations to the interests and abilities of Methodism's singers and the leaders of singing. In spite of his complaining about choirs and anthems (see page 94) and his vigorous defense of unison singing (see "Thoughts on the Power of Music" pages 84-93), he adds the florid and sectioned anthem "Cheshunt," as the final selection in the 1770 edition of *Sacred Melody*. The 1788 edition of *Sacred Harmony* includes five other anthems: THE 100 PSALM, SPRING, THE DYING CHRISTIAN, DENBIGH, and YARMOUTH. Particularly significant is the extended anthem "The Dying Christian," pages 139-47, a setting of Alexander Pope's "Dying Christians to his Soul" ("Vital spark of heavenly flame"), widely sung in Great Britain and in USA singing schools. Percy Scholes comments that this was apparently one of Wesley's favorite anthems:

On one occasion (Bolton, 1787) he says, "I desired forty or fifty children to come in and sing *Vital spark of heavenly flame*. Although some of them were silent, not being able to sing for tears, yet the harmony was such as I believe could not be equalled in the King's Chapel (Ward 1970, 632).

In addition to the inclusion of six anthems, other features of *Sacred Harmony* indicate that Wesley may have intended *Sacred Harmony* for a more musically sophisticated audience than Sacred *Melody*. For example, there are dynamic markings *pia* and *for* (*piano* and *forte*) and expression markings, such as *Andante Affecttuoso* [*sic.*] in the tune YARMOUTH, page 151. Furthermore, the collection's subtitle, "In two or three parts for the Voice, harpsichord & Organ," suggests that singing in homes or in the congregation could be supported by choirs and keyboard, although in the latter regard no figured bass is provided.

Erik Routley has provided this evaluation of the musical quality of Wesley's collections:

It is enough to say here that the implicit Methodist doctrine of hymnody seems to be this: Give us the best music we can have, but make it friendly to the people . . . [which] was the return of democracy to church-music . . . [as] it made greater use of the secular idiom (Routley 1967, 161).

### *The Contributions of Charles, Jr. and Samuel Wesley*

A generation after John Wesley's death, his nephews Charles, Jr. and Samuel made distinctive contributions to the music of Methodist congregational song. In 1822, preface dated 1821, Charles edited a harmonized and figured bass edition of *Sacred Harmony* intended "to recall the attention of our congregations to the music which animated the devotion of their forefathers, and which was sanctioned by the judgment of our venerable Founder . . . [and to] put into a form more convenient for general use . . . carefully revised and figured for organ, harpsichord, or piano forte (Wesley 1822, i, xii):

> *Sacred Harmony*, a set of Tunes Collected by the late
> Rev. John Wesley, For the use of the Congregations in
> his Connexion. An Edition carefully revised and cor-
> rected by his Nephew, Charles Wesley, Esq. Organist to
> his Majesty. London: T. Blanchard.

The collection is listed as number 358 in Frank Baker's *Union
Catalogue*. There are seven extant copies, one in Great Britain and six in
the United States.

The preface, whose author is not identified but presumed to be a
Methodist minister or other church leader, provides a glimpse of early
nineteenth-century Methodist music practice:

> The present Collection of Tunes, designed originally for
> the Methodist Congregations, having become scarce, it
> was thought that an acceptable service would be to the
> lovers of that simple melody which characterized the
> singing of the primitive Methodist by republishing
> them . . . . Certain it is, that since the airs in the "Sacred
> Harmony" have been suffered to fall into neglect or
> oblivion, the character of our congregational singing has
> not generally improved. . . . It must be lamented, that the
> rage for new tunes which was for many years indulged,
> and the eagerness with which every collection was
> bought up and introduced, deluged the Connection with
> base, dissonant, unscientific, and tasteless compositions,
> utterly destructive of that rich and solemn melody,
> which best becomes religious services, and most power-
> fully excites those emotions which act subserviently to
> edification, by giving force to the words sung, and fix-
> ing the attention more directly upon them.

> One great reason of this evil has been the inattention of
> Ministers themselves to this part of the service of the
> sanctuary; for what primitive bishops and general coun-
> cils did not think it unimportant to regulate or improve,
> has been too often left among us to the leaders of tunes

and to choirs of singers. The consequence has been, that every tune which recommended itself to a false, as vulgar, or a light taste, or which was adopted for no other reason than its novelty, has been employed to spoil the effect of the finest sacred poetry, not inspired, ever put into the lips of religious worshippers; and not unfrequently to silence whole congregations for the sake of the exhibition of the orchestra (Wesley 1822, i-ii).

The balance of the preface is a remarkable survey of Christian hymns where the writer quotes Bishop Taylor and the Eastcheap Lectures.

John's other nephew Samuel Wesley, in *Original Hymn Tunes*, 1828, composed tunes for hymns in each of the meters represented in the 1780 *Collection*. Samuel's work is a stylistic alternative to his uncle's exclusive cross-referencing of that *Collection* to the 1786 edition of *Sacred Harmony*. See pages 78-79. Erik Routley, who was apparently the first to explore the collection in *The Musical Wesleys*, pages 258-63, comments that Samuel's tunes avoid the popular style, "which brought us such trivia as the still celebrated *Sagina* and *Diadem*, [as well as] the undemonstrative which Novello advocated in *The Psalmist*, and which the new Anglican hymnody encouraged . . . [and are] the work of one of England's most influential musicians" (Routley 1968, 263).

### John Wesley, Music Critic

Wesley's opinions on music were a by-product of his disciplined reading on a variety of subjects. Albert C. Outler has commented:

> Wesley's 'worlds' were not all 'theological.' He had read enough English literature to use it freely and to form quite confident value-judgments about it that dissented from the fashions of his time and those of ours as well. Moreover, he was widely and well read in most aspects of the intellectual, cultural (and industrial and

economic) transitions of his century, and was able to bring much of this to his task as tutor to the uninstructed folk in his societies (Wesley 1984, 77).

Erik Routley in *The Musical Wesleys* provides commentary on Wesley's wide-ranging interests:

> As one reads his *Journal*, one is impressed on every page by the fact that nothing lay outside his interest; nothing new could come into his sight but it would have, for the moment, his full attention, and elicit a characteristic and wise comment. [Wesley possessed] this special faculty for observing what others merely see [and], for listening to what others passively hear (Routley 1968, 5).

Wesley's notes on his Monday, June 13, 1748, conversation in London with Johann Christoph Pepusch reveal a limited, but nevertheless essential, understanding of the development of English church music. Pepusch, 1667-1752, was a German-English opera composer and theorist, and the organist of Charterhouse.

> I spent an hour or two with Dr. Pepusch. He asserted, that the art of music is lost; that the ancients only understood it in its perfection; that it was revived a little in the reign of King Henry VIII, by Tallys [Tallis] and his contemporaries; as also in the reign of Queen Elizabeth, who was a judge and patroness of it; that after her reign it was not sung for sixty or seventy years, till Purcell made some attempts to restore it; but that ever since, the true, ancient art, depending on nature and mathematical principle, had gained no ground; the present masters having no fixed principle at all (Wesley 1872, 2:100).

Wesley's breadth of reading in music history and commentary is seen in this comment on *Essay on Musical Expression*, 1752, a treatise by the composer, organist, and music historian Charles Avison, 1709-70.

> 22 October, 1768. I was much surprised in reading an *Essay on Music*, wrote by one who is a thorough master of the subject, to find that the music of the ancients was

as simple as that of the Methodists; that their music wholly consisted of melody, or the arrangement of single notes; that what is now called harmony, singing in parts, the whole of counterpoint and fugues, is quite novel, being never known in the world till the popedom of Leo the Tenth. He further observes that, as the time necessarily prevents attention to the sense, so it frequently destroys melody for the sake of harmony; meantime it destroys the very end of music, which is to affect the passions (Wesley 1872, 5:290).

### Thoughts on the Power of Music

Wesley's most important effort to set forth his views on appropriate music for Methodists is found in his "Thoughts on the Power of Music," completed at Inverness, June 9, 1779.

1. By the power of music, I mean its power to affect the hearers; to raise various passions in the human mind. Of this we have very surprising accounts in ancient history. We are told the ancient Greek musicians in particular were able to excite whatever passions they pleased; to inspire love or hate, joy or sorrow, hope or fear, courage, fury, or despair; yet, to raise these one after another, and to vary the passions just according to the variation of the music.

2. But how is this to be accounted for? No such effects attend the modern music, although it is confessed on all hands, that our instruments excel theirs, beyond all degrees of comparison. What was their lyre, their instruments of seven or ten strings, compared to our violin? What were any of their pipes to our hautboy or German flute? What were all of them put together, all that were in use two or three thousand years ago, to our organ? How is it, then, that with this inconceivable advantage the modern music has less power than the ancient?

3. Some have given a very short answer to this, cutting the knot which they could not untie. They have doubted, or affected to doubt, the fact; perhaps they have even denied it. But no sensible man will do this, unless he be utterly blinded by prejudice. For it would be denying the faith of all history, seeing no fact is better authenticated. None is delivered down to us by more unquestionable testimony, such as fully satisfies in all other cases. We have, therefore, no more reason to doubt of the power of Timotheus's music than of Alexander's arms; and we may deny his taking Persepolis, as well as his burning it through the sudden rage which was excited in him by that musician. And the various effects which were successively wrought in his mind (so beautifully described by Dryden, in his Ode on St. Cecilia's Day) are astonishing instances of the power of a single harp to transport, as it were, the mind out of itself.

4. Nay we read of an instance, even in more modern history, of the power of music, not inferior to this. A musician being brought to the King of Denmark and asked whether he could excite any passion, answered in the affirmative, and was commanded to make the trial upon the king himself. Presently the monarch was all in tears; and upon the musician's changing his mood, he was quickly roused to such fury, that snatching a sword from one of his assistants' hands (for they had purposely removed his own) he immediately killed him, and would have killed all the room had he not been forcibly withheld.

5. This alone removes all the incredibility of what is related concerning the ancient music. But why is it that modern music, in general, has no such effect on the hearers? The grand reason seems to be no other than this—the whole nature and design of music is altered. The ancient composers studied melody alone, the due arrangement of single notes; and it was by melody alone

that they wrought such wonderful effects. And as this music was directly calculated to move the passions, so they designed it for this very end. But the modern composers study harmony, which in the present sense of the word is quite another thing—namely, a contrast of various notes, opposite to, and yet blended with each other, wherein they now high, now low, pursue the resonant fugue.

Dr. Gregory says, "This harmony has been known in the world little more than two hundred years." Be that as it may, ever since it was introduced—ever since counterpoint has been invented, as it has altered the grand design of music, so it has well-nigh destroyed its effects.

6. Some indeed have imagined, and attempted to prove, that the ancients were acquainted with this. It seems there needs but one single argument to demonstrate the contrary. We have many capital pieces of ancient music that are now in the hands of the curious. Dr. Pepusch, who was well versed in the music of antiquity (perhaps the best of any man in Europe), showed me several large Greek folios, which contained many of their musical compositions. Now is there, or is there not, any counterpoint in these? The learned know there is no such thing. There is not the least trace of it to be found: it is all melody, and no harmony.

7. And as the nature of music is thus changed, so is likewise the design of it. Our composers do not aim at moving the passions, but at quite another thing; at varying and contrasting the notes a thousand different ways. What had counterpoint to do with the passions? It is applied to a quite different faculty of the mind; not to our joy, our hope, or fear; but merely to the ear, to the imagination, or internal sense. And the pleasure it gives is not upon this principle; not by raising any passion

whatever. It no more affects the passions than the judgment: Both the one and the other lie quite out of its province.

8. Need we any other, and can we have any stronger, proof of this, than those modern overtures, voluntaries, or concertos, which consist altogether of artificial sounds without any words at all? What have any of the passions to do with these? What has judgment, reason, common sense? Just nothing at all. All these are utterly excluded by delicate, unmeaning sound!

9. In this respect the modern music has no connexion with common sense, any more than with the passions. In another, it is glaringly, undeniably, contrary to common sense: namely, in allowing, yea, appointing different words to be sung by different persons at the same time! What can be more shocking to a man of understanding than this? Pray, which of those sentences am I to attend to? I can attend only to one sentence at once and I hear three or four at one and the same instant! And, to complete the matter, this astonishing jargon has found a place even in the worship of God! It runs through (O pity! O shame!) the greatest part even of our Church music! It is found even in the finest of our anthems, and in the most solemn parts of our public worship! Let any impartial and unprejudiced person say whether there can be a more direct mockery of God.

10. But to return: Is it strange that modern music does not answer the end it is not designed for? and which it is in no wise calculated for? It is not possible that it should. Had Timotheus "pursued the resonant fugue," his music would have been quite harmless. It would have affected Alexander no more than Bucephalus; the finest city in the world had not been destroyed; but Persepolis stares, *Cyrique arx alta maneres.*

11. It is true that modern music had been sometimes observed to have as powerful an effect as the ancient, so that frequently single persons, and sometimes numerous assemblies, have been seen in a flood of tears. But when was this? Generally, if not always, when a fine solo was sung; when "the sound has been an echo to the sense"; when the music has been extremely simple and inartificial, the composer having attended to melody, not harmony. Then, and then only, the natural power of music to move the passions has appeared. This music was calculated for that end, and effectually answered it.

12. Upon this ground it is that so many persons are so much affected by Scotch or Irish airs. They are composed not according to art but nature; they are simple in the highest degree. There is no harmony, according to the present sense of the word, therein; but there is much melody. And this is not only heard, but felt, by all those who retain their native taste, whose taste is not biased (I might say corrupted) by attending to counterpoint and complicated music. It is this counterpoint, it is harmony (so-called) which destroys the power of music. And if ever this should be banished from our composition, if ever we should return to the simplicity and melody of the ancients, then the effects of our music will be as surprising as any that were wrought by theirs; yea, perhaps they will be as much greater as modern instruments are more excellent than those of the ancients (Wesley 1872, 13:470-73).

### Commentary on "The Power of Music"

1. In this paragraph Wesley states that music has the power to prompt passionate responses in the human mind, an ideal that was extended into theories of human behavior by the Swiss educator, Johann Heinrich Pestalozzi, 1746-1827, espoused in the USA by Lowell Mason

and fostered in twentieth-century music education, whereby persons can be and often are better, i.e., more disciplined and responsible, for having participated in the music-aesthetic experience. This ideal is implicit in the training of English cathedral-choirs and the nineteenth-century choral societies.

On at least one occasion, Monday, December 31, 1764, Wesley's curiosity about the power of music carried over into the animal kingdom:

> I thought it would be worth while to make an odd experiment. Remembering how surprisingly fond of music the lion at Edinburgh was, I determined to try whether this was the case with all animals of the same kind. I accordingly went to the tower with one who plays on the German flute. He began playing near four or five lions; only one of these (the rest not seeming to regard it at all) rose up, came to the front of his den, and seemed to be all attention.

> Meanwhile, a tiger in the same den started up, leaped over him again, and so to and fro incessantly. Can we account for this by any principle of mechanism? Can we account for it at all? (Wesley 1872, 3:202-03).

2. Citing the confusion of the modern composers, Wesley evidently shares Charles's conservative views as expressed in "Modern Music" and "The Pianoforte," pages 174-76. John, nevertheless, apparently approved the counterpoint in Handel's oratorio choruses. Wesley's references to musical instruments provide some insight into his musical vocabulary. The violin is probably the baroque-style instrument played in the opera-oratorio orchestras of Handel and Lampe. The hautboy, also written "hautbois" and "hoboy," is an oboe. Prior to the mid-seventeenth century it was also called a shawm. The late Roger Deschner often stated that Wesley had an oboist lead hymns during field preaching. John and Charles Wesley are reported to have played the flute, probably the recorder that is held vertically and blown from the end. The German flute, called the traverse flute because it is held transversely and blown from the side, was introduced to England in Wesley's time. The organ

he heard in parish churches, academic chapels, abbeys, and cathedrals by continental standards was a modest instrument without a pedal board. James T. Lightwood in "The Use of Stringed Instruments" and "The Chapel Orchestra," in *Stories of Methodist Music: Nineteenth Century,* describes and comments on the various instruments that apparently were used in Methodist chapels during Wesley's time. The organ and bass viol were apparently the only instruments that the Conference sanctioned.

3. Routley has pointed out Wesley's dubious linking of Timotheus' music-making to Alexander's career. In this section Wesley begins to qualify his opinion that "modern music has less power than the ancient." His reference to Dryden's "Ode on St. Cecilia's Day" is apparently to the text only. It does not reflect the possibility of his hearing the musical setting by John Blow, 1684, or G. F. Handel's choral, solo, and instrumental masterpiece composed in 1739, including the opening chorus "From Harmony, from heavenly Harmony." It is interesting that Dryden's ode extols the power of musical instruments, not music with words.

4. Wesley's account from the Danish court dramatizes his point about music's ability to arouse various human passions and is the transition to a comparison of unison and contrapuntal music—the former being the grand design of ancient music.

5. Wesley's argument for the primacy of ancient music may be based on "Essay on Musical Expression," 1752, by the composer, organist, and music historian Charles Avison, 1709-70. See quotation from Wesley's diary for October, 1768, page 83. Erik Routley states that Dr. [John] Gregory is the prominent Scotch author and teacher of medicine (Routley 1968, 23).

6. Johann Christoph Pepusch, 1667-1752, was a German-English opera composer and theorist, and organist of Charterhouse. Wesley is characteristically selective in his sources and is apparently citing Pepusch's paper on Greek music that the music historian delivered when he was named a Fellow of the Royal Society in 1746. Pepusch's

interests were not limited to unison music, but ran the gamut of ancient music including the sixteenth-century madrigal.

7. Wesley reiterates his essential point that music's fundamental power and purpose are to move the passions.

8. According to Wesley, music without words is sounds without sense.

9. For all his complaining about counterpoint, it is used in the anthems that Wesley included in the 1788 edition of *Sacred Harmony*. See page 79.

10. Wesley's reach into antiquity for support of his argument greatly moved, indeed, incensed Erik Routley:

> The quotation is an adaptation of Aeneid, II 56: *Troiaque nunc staret, Priamique arx alta maneres*, in which, with typically eighteenth-century conceit, Wesley has adapted "Troy" to the capital of Persia, and with a high hand, such as he deplored when others applied it to his own and his brother's works, altered Virgil's subtle change of person to suit the ruder needs of his own argument (Routley 1968, 22).

The Wesley *Works* editor's note reads:

> and is thus translated by Pitt:—Old Priam still his empire would enjoy, And still thy towers had stood, majestic Troy (Wesley 1872, 473).

11. While admitting some persons are moved by modern music, Wesley ranks the solo voice superior to instrumental music.

12. For Wesley the natural, simple, unison folk music of Scotland and Ireland is akin to that of the ancients. Folk music was adapted by Methodist amateur musicians, who seldom left the tunes in their primitive state, into hymn tunes Wesley included in *Sacred Melody* and *Sacred Harmony*.

13. The comments by Albert C. Outler about Wesley's sermons should be taken into account when evaluating Wesley's only written extensive opinion on music:

> It is clear enough that Wesley never expected to be edited critically; it is even probable that he would have deplored such an exercise as pedantic. His quotations are rarely exact and rarely identified; his allusions are casual and his borrowings acknowledged vaguely or not at all (Outler 1984, 75).

One should also consider Wesley's lack of expertise in music performance practice and music history and the urgent need in Methodist societies to come to grips with the increasing popularity of village singing groups and their impact on Methodist worship-song. What is difficult to excuse is Wesley's reduction of the complex matter of musical taste into music "ancient" and "modern," his selected use of contemporary conservative opinion, and the apparent contradiction in his argument for the primacy of melody while stating in other contexts his avowed attraction to that popular expression of vocal counterpoint, Handel's oratorio choruses.

Wesley's essential argument abides: congregational music ought to be simple, singable, moving, memorable, and teachable. His views continued to influence Methodists in the decades following his death. Sometimes they were invoked by the Conferences in their attempt to mediate the growing number of conflicts between singers and preachers. Lightwood comments on these tensions:

> The singers were not always ready or willing to recognize or acknowledge the authority of the pulpit. They could not bring themselves to forego their special music and their set pieces, and frequently the preacher found himself powerless to resist. But not always; sometimes he proved to be more than a match for them (Lightwood 1928, 35).

For example, at one chapel the choir refused to lead-out the hymns that were selected by the preacher, whereby the trustees replaced them with a precentor and pitchpipe. In another chapel the preacher, objecting to the tunes that the choir sang, announced at the beginning of evening service:

> You are, perhaps, surprised to see the singing-gallery empty. The fact is I have nailed up the door. I have borne with these fellows long enough, and am resolved to bear with them no longer. They shall either conduct the singing in a manner different from what they have done, or they shall not conduct at all (Lightwood 1928, 35).

The 1815 Manchester Conference made reference to Wesley's "Thoughts" in its attempt to reestablish authority in congregational song, an authority that formerly had uniquely resided in the work and witness of Methodism's founder.

> Q. 15. What directions are necessary with respect to our congregational singing?

> 3. Let the excellent paper, inserted by Mr. Wesley in the *Arminian Magazine* for 1781, and entitled "Thoughts on the Power of Music," be immediately reprinted in the magazine, and also published in a separate form, that copies may be sent to every Circuit. And let the Preachers promote, as much as possible, the restoration (in our public singing) of the style of music which that paper recommends, and which is exemplified in many of our best and oldest tunes (Lightwood 1928, 35-36).

### Wesley's Additional Opinions on Music

Wesley demonstrates a working knowledge of aesthetics in the sermon "Spiritual Idolatry," where he compares music and poetry:

> 11. But is not chiefly to novelty that we are to impute the pleasure we receive from music. Certainly this has an

intrinsic beauty, as well as frequently an intrinsic grandeur. This is a beauty and grandeur of a peculiar kind, not easy to be expressed; nearly related to the sublime and the beautiful in poetry, which give an exquisite pleasure. And yet it may be allowed that novelty heightens the pleasure which arises from any of these sources (Wesley 1986, 3:109).

Wesley instinctively applied what he heard and read to Methodist music and performance practice, primarily hymns and hymn singing. He often expressed concern for the standardization of hymn singing performance practice under the broader topic of formality in worship. This concern is seen in this excerpt from the "Large" *Minutes*, Wesley's wide-ranging conversations with Methodist preachers, some as early as 1746 (Lightwood 1927, 18), that he reduced into questions and answers.

Q 39. How shall we guard against formality in public worship; particularly in singing? A. (1) By preaching frequently on the head. (2) By taking care to speak only what we feel. (3) By choosing such hymns as are proper for the congregation. (4) By not singing too much at once; seldom more than five or six verses. (5) By suiting the tune to the words. (6) By often stopping short and asking the people, "Now, do you know what you said last? Did you speak no more than you felt?" Is not this formality creeping in already, by those complex [anthems and fuging] tunes, which it is scarcely possible to sing with devotion? Besides, it is a flat contradiction to our Lord's command, "Use not vain repetitions." For what is a vain repetition, if this is not? What end of devotion does it serve? Sing no anthems. (7) Do not suffer the people to sing too slow. This naturally tends to formality, and is brought in by them who have either very strong or very weak voices. (8) In every large society let them learn to sing; and let them always learn our own tunes first. (9) Let the women constantly sing their parts alone. Let no man sing with them, unless he understands the notes, and sings the bass, as it is pricked down in the book. (10) Introduce no new tunes, till they are perfect in the old. (11) Let no organ be placed anywhere, till proposed in the Conference. (12) Recommend our tune-book everywhere; and if you cannot sing yourself choose a person or two in each place to pitch the tune for you. (13) Exhort every one in the congregation to sing, not one in ten only. (14) If a Preacher be present, let no singer give out the words. (15) When they would teach a tune to the congregation, they must sing only the tenor. After the preaching, take a little lemonade, mild ale, or candied orange-peel. All spirituous liquors, at that time especially, are deadly poison (*Minutes* 1862, 1:529-33).

Lightwood cites discussions about singing at the 1765 Conference in Dublin:

Q. Might not some parts of the late Conference in Dublin be of use to us?

A. They might: which therefore are subjoined.

Q. What can be done to make the people sing better?

A. (1) Teach them to sing by note and to sing our tunes first. (2) Take care that they do not sing too slow. (3) Exhort all that can, in every congregation, to sing. (4) Set them right that sing wrong. Be patient herein.

When the 1768 Bristol Conference discussed the work of the preachers, responsibilities for overseeing music was included in section 6:

Beware of formality in singing, as it will creep in upon us unawares. Is it not creeping in by those complex tunes which it is impossible to sing with devotion? Such is, "Praise the Lord, ye blessed ones!" Such the long quavering Hallelujah annexed to the Morning-Song tune [page 29 in Sacred Melody], which I defy any man living to sing devoutly. The repeating the same words so often (but especially while another repeats different words, the horrid abuse which runs through the modern church-music), as it shocks all common sense, so it necessarily brings in dead formality, and has no more of religion in it than a Lancashire hornpipe. Besides, it is a flat contradiction to our Lord's command, "Use not vain repetitions." For what is a vain repetition, if this is not? What end of devotion does it serve?

Is it not possible that all Methodists in the nation should sing equally quick? Why should not the Assistant see that they be taught to sing in every large Society? And do this in such a manner as to obviate the ill effects which might otherwise spring therefrom? (Lightwood 1927, 35-36).

While Wesley's views and interests were primarily in hymn tunes and congregational song, they also included choirs and their performances, organs and organists, and music history, criticism, and church music:

[Bristol, Thursday, August 17, 1758] I went to the cathedral to hear Mr. Handel's *Messiah*. I doubt if that congregation was ever so serious at a sermon as they were during this performance. In many parts, especially some of the choruses, it exceeded my expectation (Wesley 1872, 2:456).

[Wednesday, February 29, 1764] I heard *Judith*, an oratorio, performed at the Lock. Some parts of it were exceeding fine; but there are two things in all modern pieces of music which I could never reconcile to common sense.

One is singing the same words ten times over; the other, singing different words by different persons, at one and the same time. And this in the most solemn addresses to God, whether by way of prayer or of thanksgiving. This can never be defended by all the musicians in Europe, till reason is quite out of date (Wesley 1872, 3:160-61).

[Neath, Thursday, August 9, 1768] I began reading prayers at six, but was greatly disgusted at the manner of singing: (1) twelve or fourteen persons kept it to themselves, and quite shut out the congregation; (2) these repeated the same words, contrary to all sense and reason, six or eight or ten times over; (3) according to the shocking custom of modern music, different persons sung different words at one and the same moment; an intolerable insult on common sense, and utterly incompatible with any devotion (Wesley 1872, 3:339).

[Thursday, March 19, 1778] In the evening, I preached at Pubworth church; but I seemed out of my element. A long anthem was sung; but I suppose none beside the singers could understand one word of it. Is not that "praying in an unknown tongue"? I could no more bear it in any church of mine than Latin prayers (Wesley 1872, 4:116).

Wesley censored the singing that he heard at Warrington on Sunday, April 8, 1781.

The service was at the usual hours. I came just in time to put a stop to a bad custom, which was creeping in here; a few men, who had fine voices, sang a psalm which no one knew, in a tune fit for an opera, wherein three, four, or five persons sang different words at the same time! What an insult upon common sense! What a burlesque upon public worship! No custom can excuse such a mixture of profaneness and absurdity (Wesley 1872, 4:200).

As late as the Manchester Conference of 1787, Wesley expresses his opinion that anthems and presumably choirs were divisive (see answer 6 to question 39 in "Large" *Minutes*):

> No anthems be in future allowed in Methodist chapels,
> because they cannot "be properly called joint worship"
> (Smith 1866, 1:547).

James T. Lightwood comments that Wesley's view, in spite of widespread use of anthems particularly in the North and Midland's chapels, was apparently maintained by the Conference until 1796, five years after his death. At that Conference "the old resolution concerning the singing of anthems underwent a slight modification, and was reproduced in this form:"

> Let no anthems be introduced into our chapels (unless
> on extraordinary occasions and with the consent of the
> Assistant) because they cannot properly be called joint-
> worship.
>
> Also we agree with our late Rev. Father that our own
> tunes should be learned and sung in preference to oth-
> ers, as in these the whole congregation can in general
> join (Lightwood 1928, 9).

For additional comment on Wesleyan singing-practice, see pages 59-66.

Concerning organs and organists Wesley had mixed views:

> [Easter Day, April 7, 1751 at Manchester] After preach-
> ing, I went to the new church, and found an uncommon
> blessing, at a time when I least expected it, namely,
> while the organist was playing a voluntary! (Wesley
> 1872, 2:226).

The editor of Wesley's *Journal* includes an account from the *Primitive Methodist Magazine*, March 1850, about Wesley's confrontation in Louth, Lincolnshire, after he had introduced the hymn "I thirst, thou wounded Lamb of God." Wesley was distracted by the organ and after the first stanza said, "Let that organ stop, and let the women take their parts." "They cannot sing without, sir," replied Mr. Robinson. [To which Wesley retorted] "Then, how did they do before they got one?" (Wesley 1872, 7:411n).

Wesley's visit to Exeter cathedral, Sunday, August, 29, 1762, according to Erik Routley, may also have been "the first time John heard a swell box" (Routley 1968, 11):

> At the cathedral we had a useful sermon, and the whole service was performed with great seriousness and decency. Such an organ I never saw or heard before, so large, so beautiful, and so finely toned; and the music of "Glory to God in the highest," I think, exceeded the *Messiah* itself (Wesley 1872, 3:111).

Wesley recorded another favorable impression of organ playing at Macclesfield, during the Good Friday service, March 29, 1782:

> We administered the sacrament to about thirteen hundred persons. While we were administering I heard a low, soft, solemn sound, just like that of an harp. It continued five or six minutes, and so affected many that they could not refrain from tears. It then gradually died away. Strange that no other organist (that I know) should think of this. In the evening, I preached at our Room. Here was that harmony which art cannot imitate (Wesley 1872, 4:223).

See also pages 64-65 for Wesley's 1757 account of singing practices of Methodists compared with those of the established church for another negative opinion about organ voluntaries.

Wesley's injunction about organs in Methodist worship practice, included in his "Large" *Minutes* (11), "Let no organ be placed anywhere, till proposed in the Conference," was apparently ignored, according to James T. Lightwood:

> At least three organs were erected in his preaching-houses during Wesley's lifetime, the most important

> being the instrument erected in the New King Street
> Chapel, Bath, soon after its opening in 1779. . . .
> Organs were also erected in the chapels (Wesley pre-
> ferred the name 'preaching-house') in Newark and
> Keighley (Lightwood 1927, 40).

Wesley's resistance to the inclusion of organs in Methodist worship
stemmed from British evangelicals who set themselves apart from
Anglican worship practice and from the Puritanical perception of the
organ's entertainment qualities. Another reason was the cost of the
instrument, as Nicholas Temperley has summarized:

> An organ in this period cost several hundred pounds to
> buy, and an annual sum of £20 or so to pay the organ-
> ist, with perhaps a further £5 to cover tuning, minor
> repairs, and the wages of the bellows blower. In all the
> equivalent of £1000 in capital was about the minimum
> that would be required. Such a sum was beyond the
> means of all but the wealthiest parishes, and it was by
> no means clear that parish funds could legally be used
> for this purpose (Temperley 1979, 105).

In *Sacred Harmony*, 1780, Wesley accommodated the societies'
increasing use of keyboard instruments to accompany solo and congregational singing, as shown in the subtitle: "Set to Music in two and three
parts for the Voice, Harpsichord & Organ." For parallel developments in
evangelical chapels and Anglican parishes see Temperley 1979, 214-16.

The apparent widespread use of instruments in Methodist worship
in Wesley's time was cited by John Stephens, president of the Methodist
Conference, in his December 9, 1827 *Address to the Methodists of
Leeds*, delivered during the "Leeds organ controversy."

> Now what is the cause of all this strife in Leeds? An
> Organ!—Not a question whether it is proper to use
> Instrumental Music in God's Worship; for that is settled
> long ago. I myself remember the employment of musi-
> cal instruments in a Methodist Chapel nearly 50 years

ago. How long you have had Instruments of Music in your chapels at Leeds I do not know; but to my knowledge you have had them many years. The question is not between Vocal and Instrumental Music, but between one species of Instrumental Music and another (Stephens 1827, 15-16).

### *Developments Following Wesley's Death*

James T. Lightwood in *Stories of Methodist Music: Nineteenth Century* documents the increasing use of choirs, organs, and instruments in Methodist chapels after Wesley's death in 1791. For example, groups of singers and instrumentalists often performed at special services such as charity benefits. Some ministers objected that the musicians took up too much time, a complaint that was taken up by the 1800 Conference at Wesley's City Road Chapel, London:

> Q. 15. Can anything be done to prevent what appears to us to be a great evil, namely Bands of Music and theatrical singers being brought into our chapels, when charity sermons are to be preached?

> A. Let none in our Connexion preach charity sermons where such persons and such music are introduced. And let the Stewards, Trustees and Leaders be informed that such a practice is offensive to the Conference, who believe it has been hurtful to the minds of many pious people (Lightwood 1928, 27).

The Conference's action did little to stop the activity of choirs that

> were eager to to extend their choral activities beyond the range of the ordinary hymn-tune, but the congregation appreciated the anthem, or "set piece," as it was then called. Music of this kind was not lacking, for in addition to Handel's choruses and anthems by Kent, Mason,

and others, contemporary composers were also writing music that met with great popularity.

[For example] At the opening of Bridge Street Wesleyan Chapel, Bolton, by the Rev. Samuel Bradburn in 1803, the choir had arranged to sing as their anthem "The horse and his rider hath he thrown into the sea." This was duly performed with trumpets, horns, violins, hautboys, bassoons, bass viols and double bass, to the obvious delight of the performers, but the equally evident annoyance of the preacher. At length he could stand it no longer, and, turning to the eager musicians he exclaimed in a voice of amazing power: "I say! put that horse in the stable; we've had enough of him for one day." The astonished musicians promptly subsided, quite overawed for the time by the preacher's voice and manner (Lightwood 1928, 27-28).

The 1805 Conference held at Sheffield also dealt with the apparent widespread use of choirs and instruments.

Q. 20. Are there regulations necessary with regard to singing?

A. 1. Let no instruments of music be introduced into the singers' seats, except a bass viol, should the principal singer require it.

2. Let no books of hymns be henceforth used in our chapels, except the hymn-books printed for our Book-Room.

3. Let no *Pieces*, as they are called, in which *recitatives*, by single men, solos, by single women, fuguing (or different words sung by different voices at the same time) are introduced, be sung in our chapels.

4. Let the original, simple, grave and devotional style be carefully preserved, which, instead of drawing the attention to singing and the singers, is so admirable calculated to draw off the attention from both, and raise the soul to God only.

5. Let no musical Festivals, or, as they are sometimes termed, Selections of Sacred Music, be either encouraged or permitted in any of our chapels: in which performances the genuine dignity of spiritual worship is grossly abused under the pretense of getting money for charitable purposes; which, we have sufficient proof, has been procured as amply where nothing of the kind has been introduced, but the charity recommended to the people in the name of God.

7. Let no Preacher, therefore, suffer his right to conduct every part of the worship of Almighty God to be infringed on, either by the singers or others.

Lightwood comments on the shaping of this instruction:

It is evident that the brethren who then assembled in Conference did not invite the assistance of a musician in framing their regulations, hence the distinction they drew between "recitative" and "solo" is scarcely in accordance with the generally accepted meanings of those terms (Lightwood 1928, 28-29).

### *John Wesley and Popular Music*

Methodism's tune repertory was greatly expanded in John Wesley's collections to include those composed or adapted to accommodate the increasing number of meters in Charles Wesley's hymns: folk tunes; vocal and instrumental melodies from Italian opera and Handelian sacred and secular oratorio; and highly ornamented melody scored in basso-continuo solo social style and accompanied by a viol or string bass, organ or harpsichord. The latter repertory was introduced to Methodists in John F. Lampe's settings of twenty-three texts by Charles and one by his brother Samuel Wesley in *Hymns on the Great Festivals and Other Occasions*, 1746. See pages 105-11 for commentary on this collection. See also Robin Leaver's survey of tunes that Methodists probably sang prior to Lampe's collection in "Lampe's tunes," facsimile reprint *Hymns on the Great Festivals and Other Occasions*, 1746, the Charles Wesley Society, 1995.

The inclusion of Lampe's tunes in Wesley's collections and John Wesley's adaptation of the popular music of his day have led some in their time period to justify their use of pop music by quoting what have been assumed to be John Wesley's words, "Why should the Devil have all the good tunes?" While it is apparent that Wesley included a wide range of music in his collections, there is no evidence that he ever used this phrase to justify using a variety of music, some of it traditional, much of it composed by those whom Wesley favored and closely super-vised. This writer is indebted to Nicholas Temperley and Frank Baker who have narrowed the source of this oft-quoted phrase to E. W. Broome's book published in 1881, on the Anglican clergyman Rowland Hill, 1744-1833, a critic of John Wesley. Broome says of Hill, "He did not see any reason why the devil should have all the good tunes" (Partington, 1992, 338).

Popular music for Wesley's educated constituents meant the arias and occasional music of opera and oratorio, the broadsheet ballad (see Leaver 1994, 5) and the parlor song, folk music combined with dance, and concerts. On one occasion Wesley attended a concert in Southampton by "the famous musician that plays upon the [tuned] glasses," and Wesley's presence caused "an heap of Gentry" to attend his preaching in the evening (Wesley 1872, 4:391).

It is well documented that he attended and apparently enjoyed Handel's oratorio, but not all forms of popular music were acceptable to him. For example, the *masquerade* successfully produced by John F. Lampe was criticized by Wesley in "A Farther Appeal to Men of Reason and Religion," 1745, as his generation's rejection of traditional British values:

Temperance, patience, and scorn of superfluities, the rough, indefatigable industry [that have been] exchanged for softness, "idleness, and fullness of bread" [Ezek. 16:49] (Wesley 1975, 231).

In his *Foundery Collection*, 1742, *Sacred Melody*, appended to *Select Hymns with Tunes Annext*, 1761, and *Sacred Harmony*, 1780, Wesley included excerpts from opera and oratorio. An example of the former is JERICHO TUNE, adapted from G. F. Handel's *Ricardo Primo*, 1727, first included on page five of the *Foundery Collection*, 1742, and apparently transcribed from the first violin part and scored more than an octave above the singers' range. Methodist societies also used Thomas Butts's *Harmonia Sacra*, ca. 1756, which included many tunes adapted from instrumental and theater sources: nine tunes from Handel's operas and oratorios, two from Arne's operas, and two from Lampe's *Ladies Amusement* in addition to twenty-two in theater-song style from *Hymns on the Great Festivals and Other Occasions*, 1746. Apparently Wesley tolerated the societies' use of these tunes until he published his second tune book, *Sacred Melody*, appended to *Select Hymns with Tunes Annext*, 1761, and taking a cue from Butts, he incorporated a number of theater melodies, including Henry Purcell's tune in *King Arthur*, 1691, for John Dryden's "Fairest isle, all isles excelling" as a setting for Charles Wesley's "Love divine, all loves excelling." Charles, whose hymn's structure, phraseology and language reflects Dryden's poem, apparently intended it to be sung to Purcell's tune.

### *John (Johann) F. Lampe, Methodism's first composer*

John F. Lampe's twenty-four tunes in *Hymns on the Great Festivals and Other Occasions*, 1746, is the most compelling example of Methodist appropriation of popular music, in this instance the theater song. The importance of this work caused Lightwood to distinguish Lampe as "the First Methodist Composer" in chapter 5, *Methodist Music in the Eighteenth Century,* 1927.

In the introduction to the facsimile reprint of *Hymns on the Great Festivals and Other Occasions*, 1746, this writer has provided a biography of Lampe and an account of his interactions with the Wesleys. The following is taken from portions of that work and is included with permission from the Charles Wesley Society.

John Frederick Lampe was born in either 1702 or 1703, probably in Saxony, Germany. He was educated in schools near Brunswick and at the University of Helmstedt where he received a law degree. Little is known of his musical education and activity. He moved to Hamburg in 1720 and there probably began his association with G. F. Handel and introduction to Italian opera. In either 1725 or 1726 he went London where he played bassoon in Handel's orchestra at the King's Theatre. Lampe became respected as a performer, teacher, theorist (*A Plain and Compendious Method of Teaching Thorough Bass,* 1737, and *The Art of Musick,* 1740), and composer of satires and burlesque for the theater. His most successful work was the comic fantasy *The Dragon of Wantley,* 1738.

The early 1740's were uncertain times for Lampe. At this point in his career he met the Wesleys through Mrs. Rich, the former Priscilla Stevens, a convert of the Wesleys and a bit player at Covent Garden. See pages 143-46.

Charles Wesley's daughter, Eliza, describes Mrs. Rich as

> impressed with the deep seriousness by the preaching of my dear Father, who became her intimate friend; upon which she gave up the stage entirely, and suffered much reproach from her husband, who insisted on her appearing again upon it. She said, if she did appear on the stage again, it would be to bear her public testimony against it. In consequence of this declaration she escaped further importunity. She was afterward a widow, and lived in affluence. When I was young, we used to visit her at Chelsea. She was a beautiful and most amiable woman, and retained her affection to my Father and Mother during her long life (Lightwood 1927, 25).

Charles's son Samuel in the preface to *Original Hymn Tunes*, 1828, comments on his father's relationship to Lampe:

> The late Charles [*sic.*] Frederick Lampe, a Native of Germany, and an accomplished Musician, at the Solicitation of my Father, The Revd. Charles Wesley, who had an extreme regard for him, furnished an admirable Set of Tunes, fitted to several of the Metres, and which in the Author's Time were in high Estimation and general use (Wesley 1828, iii).

John Wesley's contact with Lampe is evidenced in his *Journal* for Friday, November 29, 1745:

> I spent an hour with Mr. Lampe, who had been a Deist for many years, till it pleased God, by the *Earnest Appeal [to Men of Reason and Religion*, 1743] to bring him to a better mind (Curnock 1938, 3:226).

It is quite possible (Martin 1985, 73) that Charles's poem "The Musician's Hymn," number 25 in *Hymns for those that seek and those that have Redemption in the Blood of Jesus Christ* (London, 1747) (see pages 178-80), was composed to celebrate the composer's conversion.

Charles writes of his contact with Mrs. Rich in 1746 in his *Journal* for March 29, Holy Saturday, 1746 (see page 144). In the same year Mrs. Rich in a letter to Charles states that she had shared at least one of Charles's hymns with Lampe. The excerpt also reflects Lampe's feelings toward Charles:

> I am infinitely obliged to you for your kind letter. It gave me great comfort, and at the time I had much need for it; for I have been very ill, both in body and mind. Some part arose from my poor partner, who, I fear, has in a great measure stifled his convictions which God gave him. . . . I gave a copy of the hymn to Mr. Lampe, who at the reading, shed

some tears, and said he would write to you for he loved you as well as if you were his own brother (Gill 1964, 120-21).

*Hymns on the Great Festivals and Other Occasions*, 1746, was most likely a collaborative work of Charles Wesley and Lampe. Some deem it probable that Lampe published it at his own expense (Baker 1962, 82) as a gesture of appreciation for the friendship and support of John and Charles Wesley and other Methodists whom Mrs. Rich entertained in her home and introduced to him and his wife. The tunes may have been first performed in John Rich's home in Chelsea.

Frank Baker's general article in the volume's facsimile reprint documents the collection's approximate publication date and its two-schilling price in an advertisement, "Hymns on the Great Festivals, with music and tunes," in *The Gentleman's Magazine* for October 1746.

Charles Wesley evidently endorsed Lampe's settings, seen in this response written in Newcastle to criticism of Lampe's tunes:

> Tell Mrs. Dewal not to mind that envious gentleman who slandered Lampe. His tunes are universally admired here among the musical men, and have brought me into high favour with them. (*Journal* Appendix: Selections from Correspondence, "To the Same" [My very dear Friend], Newcastle, December 11, 1746) (Wesley 1950, 2:174).

Lampe traveled to Ireland in 1749, and then to Edinburgh where he conducted and produced his works. He died July 25, 1751. Charles Wesley composed a memorial to him (see pages 180-81).

Charles and John Wesley apparently encouraged the use of Lampe's tunes. Charles wrote his wife Sally:

> How many of Lampe's tunes can you play? I am offered an exceeding fine harpsichord for sixteen guineas! What encouragement do you give me to purchase it for you? (Selections from Correspondence, letter to Sally Gwynne, March 29 [no year, presumed to be in early 1750's], (Wesley 1849, 2:184).

And John wrote Charles:

> If Mr. Lampe's tunes [possibly the 1753 reprint of *Festival Hymns*] are in print already, it is enough. I wish you had told me this six months ago, and the rest (which only we want) should have been printed before now. Pray send them by Michael Fenwick to me here. He will be in Bristol next week (June 20, 1755, letter to Charles) (Telford 1931, 3:130).

Charles also suggested that some of Lampe's tunes be used with selections in *Graces Before Meat*, ca. 1746, and he referenced Lampe's tunes to three hymns in his *Redemption Hymns*, 1747 (Lightwood 1927, 23). He apparently continued a close relationship with the Lampes. Charles records on April 27, 1747:

> That I might abstain from all appearance of evil, particularly of pride and resentment, I took up my cross, and went in Mrs. Rich's coach to Chelsea. I passed an hour or two at Lampe's, before I waited upon one who was once my friend (Wesley 1950, 1:451).

While in Dublin in 1750, John Wesley records that he sang "Happy Magdalene" with Mrs. Pilkington (Wesley 1909 3:464), presumably using Lampe's tune.

The importance of Lampe's work for our study is that his tunes are by a recognized composer of popular music who set them in a performance style that, unlike the core of tunes included in most eighteenth-century evangelical tune books, were intended for performance by soloists of demonstrated competence. They may have been written for and first performed by Lampe's wife, Isabella Lampe, a leading operatic soprano. The figured bass indicates that they were to be accompanied at the harpsichord and cello, in contrast to the melody-only format of the *Foundery Collection*, 1742. Further, they were probably intended to be performed for an affluent audience, including theater musicians and patrons, that the Wesleys had followed westward from the city. Charles Wesley's association with this group continued into the 1770's as he promoted his sons' musical careers (see pages 171-74).

Lampe's tunes that were composed in a context of London nobility and wealth were subsequently sung in Methodist societies. In some they were performed by solo voices in their original settings, and in other circumstances they were sung in congregational style as they appeared in Thomas Butts's *Harmonia Sacra*, ca. 1754, and John Wesley's *Sacred Melody*, 1761. In the latter Wesley modified Lampe's florid tunes, printing them without their original figured bass to make them more suitable for congregational singing. In *Sacred Harmony*, 1780, they were harmonized, as shown in the collection's subtitle, "In two or three parts for the Voice, Harpsichord & Organ," but the figured bass was not restored.

Nicholas Temperley's *Hymn Tune Index,* tracing tunes in English language hymnals from the mid-sixteenth century through 1820, documents the inclusion of Lampe's tunes and their variants in numerous collections. For example, INVITATION (with other names including KENT, DEVONSHIRE, BANBURY, and WILTON) appears in more than 200 collections, reprints, and revisions. Only two tunes from the 1746 collection are included in recent hymnals: INVITATION and DYING STEPHEN. For a discussion of Lampe's tunes and their use in other collections see Robin Leaver, "Lampe's tunes," facsimile reprint of *Hymns on the Great Festivals and Other Occasions*, 1746, to be published by the Charles Wesley Society.

The collection prompts more than musicological or hymnological interest. Lampe's tunes enlarged, enriched, and created a new dimension of "music of the heart" and are an expression of the movement's zeal to preach the good news to all who will listen. Their sustained use by Methodists and others demonstrate that Methodist music and music-making in Wesley's time was more stylistically diverse than previously thought, a by-product of the revival's four-decade expansion into audiences with diverse musical tastes and abilities.

The other repertory of popular song that Wesley included in his collections consisted of tunes derived from or composed after British folk melody; the latter included "Nancy Dawson" to which Charles Wesley wrote "The True Use of Musik" (see "Charles Wesley, Music Critic," pages 169-89). Wesley's collections also include a surprising number of minor or modal melodies, as well as German chorales and traditional melodies.

Another collection of Charles Wesley's texts set to theater-style tunes is Jonathan Battishill's *Twelve Hymns*, ca. 1770 (see page 171).

An interesting application of Wesley's use of popular-style tunes is found in the Lock Hospital collections of psalms and hymns (1762-94). Martin Madan, an early associate of John Wesley, was hospital chaplain and music director of its chapel. He formed the congregation as the choir because at Lock, unlike the Foundling and Magdalen Hospitals with choirs composed of inmates, the patients—men, women, and children— were frail victims of venereal disease, many of whom

> were too ill to attend chapel at all. . . . Those who were
> well enough . . . could not be displayed to the congrega-
> tion in pretty uniforms, as [children were] at the
> Foundling Hospital, or even heard singing behind can-
> vas screens, as [repentant women were] at the
> Magdalen. They were not "respectable." . . .  At the
> Lock Hospital, then, the inmates could not sing effec-
> tively on their own behalf. The congregation must sing
> for them, . . . [and] it would be necessary to persuade the
> congregation itself, or some part of it, to submit to musi-
> cal training and rehearsal, . . . [a practice] strongly held
> by . . . the Wesleys, and several other early Methodist
> leaders, who themselves were highly musical, and
> believed in the emotional power of music to promote
> religious feeling. It is no accident, therefore, that
> Methodism was a strong force in the activities of the
> Lock Hospital (Temperley, 1993, 48).

Madan and others, including the celebrated Italian Felice Giardini, composed hymns in tuneful two-part settings with the melody in the upper voice, accompanied at the organ. This repertory and performance practice also entered evangelical Anglican parish worship where the con-gregation was gradually beginning to sing hymns, though the practice was officially prohibited. Nicholas Temperley has commented:

> It was through the hospital collections the new type of
> tune, which we may call the "Methodist" type, began to

find its way into the parish churches, together with some of the hymn texts that went with it (Temperley 1979, 211).

Madan in his book *Thelyphthora*, 1780, advocated bigamy as a preferable and biblical alternative to prostitution. The ensuing scandal forced him to live in seclusion in Epsom, where he died in 1790.

### *Summary*

The role that John Wesley, a natural but untrained musician, played in shaping the repertory, performance practice, and taste of Methodist music well into the nineteenth century is seen in his remark made shortly after the publication of *Sacred Melody*. Wesley comments in his *Journal* concerning his preference for simple memorable tunes:

> I was reflecting on an odd circumstance, which I cannot account for. I never relish a tune at first hearing, not till I have almost learned to sing it; and, as I learn it more perfectly, I gradually lose my relish for it (July 3, 1764).

This confession prompted Erik Routley's wry comment on Wesley's untutored taste and indirectly is a characterization of eighteenth-century Methodist music and music making:

> Few people mention it, but this is actually the condition in which most, if not all, non-technically minded people approach the arts; they suspect, they enjoy, they cool off. It may have been hard for people to work with so strenuous a person as John Wesley when their own specialties were concerned; this was simply because, being himself no specialist in any ordinary discipline, Wesley remained to the end of his days a strictly normal figure writ large. He carried all the mediocrities and prejudices and half-formed opinions and impatiences of the "layman" into everything he turned his hand to, as well as all the flexibility that marks off the layman from the pedant. There he would advise, in music as in other matters, not what he imagined the ordinary

men would need, but what he himself needed, backing his opinion that he was himself an ordinary man in all things except in the work he had been divinely appointed to do. The whole point of his preaching was that what had happened to him in his conversion could happen to anybody who would allow it to happen. "Universal salvation" was the spiritual charter of the common man; the denial of Calvinist spiritual aristoçracy (Routley 1968, 25-26).

John Wesley as Methodism's first music editor and arbiter of taste and performance practice set the course for generations of Wesleyan and other groups' music making—the music of the heart: singable, teachable, memorable, functional, and accessible to all. Nicholas Temperley has commented that Methodists "established a new type of tune that was popular and strongly secular in style" (Temperley 1979, 212-13) that lay between the florid tunes of Lampe and the anthems of the singing school and village choirs, tunes that appealed to the average singers and suited their needs and abilities—regardless of social status. For example, Wesley's success in using popular melody among the poor inspired Martin Madan to compile the Lock Hospital collections, which provided "singing that would attract the rich and fashionable and induce them to support the Lock Hospital with their charity" (Temperley 1993, 63).

In his remarkable career as music editor, publisher, and commentator Wesley is the paradigmatic enabler of that brand of vital evangelical song that combines the singable, the heartfelt, and the appropriate—a repertory that since his time has often been the enigma and sometimes nemesis of clergy and church musician alike.

# 5. Charles Wesley: Lyrical Theologian and Music Critic

## *Charles Wesley's Musicality*

There is little evidence of Charles's musical training. We can assume, however, that he shared his brother's experiences of psalm singing in the Epworth rectory and hearing the choir of the Epworth parish church of St. Andrew. As a student in Westminster School, adjacent to Westminster Abbey, he participated in the abbey's worship life and presumably learned to appreciate, by way of the choir and organist William Croft, the cathedral choral tradition. Here the psalms in *The Book of Common Prayer* continued to be formed in his memory, attested by his use of sixty-seven psalm passages from it in the 114 poems in *Short Hymns on Select Passages of Holy Scripture*, 1762. At Christ Church, Oxford, as a founder of the Holy Club and the first to be called "Methodist," he sang Watts's metrical paraphrases using the 1708 musical supplement to the Tate and Brady psalter.

Charles's attraction to the Moravians' hymns and their music is no less than his brother's. It is usually overlooked that his conversion preceded by three days John's, and that Charles's transforming experience was expressed in his first evangelical song, "Where shall my wondering soul begin" (**342**).

Charles's musical-liturgical interests were formed in Anglican parish, abbey, collegiate, and cathedral worship. During his residencies in Bristol and London these interests were increasingly influenced by parish worship. During his twenty-two-year residence in Bristol, sixteen years probably at No. 19 Charles Street and the balance at No. 4 Charles Street (Brown 1993), he and his family attended St. James Church, now closed, as well as the cathedral. After the move to London in 1771, they worshipped at the Marylebone parish church (demolished in 1949), where he and Sally had been married, close to their home at No. 1 Great Chesterfield Street (now Wesley Street).

This excerpt from Charles's younger son Samuel's *Autobiography* provides insight into his father's musical experiences:

> My father was extremely fond of music, and in the early part of life, I believe, performed a little on the flute. . . . He had a most accurate ear for time. . . . He had not a vocal talent, but could join in a hymn or simple melody tolerable well in tune. . . . My father used to say of my brother and me, "The boys have music by their mother's" [Sarah Gwynne] (Baker 1962, 177).

Frederick C. Gill gives this assessment of Charles's musicality:

> [Charles] had a fine ear, and a passion for old church music, and for Handel whom it is probable he had met at the house of Mrs. Rich. But apart from flute-playing in his Oxford days there is no evidence of his talent with any other instrument, though his sweet-toned organ is pre-served at City Road Chapel and it is difficult not to think that he played on it (Gill 1964, 192).

The poet's *Journal* which he kept from 1736 to 1756, is invaluable for tracing his opinions on music, hymns and hymn singing, and music-hymnic performance practice in early Methodist worship. The excerpts from the *Journal*, (see pages 122-52) demonstrate the integral relation-ship of music and preaching and the need for Methodist preachers to have a strong and in some regard a trained voice.

W. L. Doughty has commented on Charles's speaking and singing voice:

> [His] voice was also one of his great assets. He records how, at Bristol, he preached to a congregation that "filled the valley and sides of a hill like grasshoppers for multi-tude. Yet my voice reached the most distant, as I perceived them bowing at the Holy name. God gave me the voice of a trumpet and sent the word home to many hearts." He had

also a fine singing voice, and occasionally, during his sermon, he sang verses that emphasized the message he was delivering (Doughty 1958, 266).

### The Music in Charles Wesley's Hymns

Since Charles seldom makes reference to his musical abilities, we usually depend upon the recollections of his son Samuel (see page 116) that attribute the musical instincts of the two sons to their mother, Sally (see page 116). However, in one poem (see page 183) Charles affirms his own musicality and appreciation for performed music as he wonders why he never received formal training. The poem's opening lines are included here:

> Ye powers who guide my actions, tell
> Why I, in whom the seeds of music dwell,
> Who most its power and excellence admire,
> Whose very breast itself a lyre
> Was never taught the happy art
> Of modulating sounds

Frank Baker appears to be the first to focus on the music in Charles's hymns, a musical instinct that combined with Sally's and was transmitted to his sons, Charles and Samuel, and his grandson, Samuel Sebastian.

> There is more of the mystery of music in many of Charles Wesley's hymns than is at first obvious, especially when the ear is deafened by a familiar tune (Baker 1988, 80).

> Although he [Wesley] could make no great musical claims as vocalist, instrumentalist, or composer, his musical sons acknowledged that his ear was impeccable [see page 116]. And because there was music in his soul, lilting, rapturous, divine music, he could not be confined to the humdrum in verse. The lyric was his *métier*. Both his inventiveness and his mastery in lyrical form were without parallel in the verse of that century, and perhaps only paralleled by Shelley in the century that followed (Baker 1988, 68).

Baker comments on how the poet's musical imagination is expressed in rhyming patterns, particularly the

> cross-rhyming double long metre ("O thou who camest from above" **[501]**) in its original double form, the double short metre ("Soldiers of Christ arise" **[513]** and other magnificent marching poems), and the double common metre ("All praise to our redeeming Lord" **[554]** and "Sing to the great Jehovah's praise" in their original double form). The production here ranges from just over to just under thirteen thousand lines each (Baker 1988, 70-71).

Wesley's alternating iambic and trochaic meters, the rising and falling beat (its musical equivalents—syncopation and cross rhythms), according to Baker stem from his contact with the Moravians (Baker 1988, 75).

> Any musician knows that if he remains in the same key for too long monotony sets in. This he avoids by modulations, passages in a different though related key, passages short or long, obvious or subtly concealed beneath the melody, varying both with the occasion and with the technical command and musical sensitivity of the composer. The same kind of thing is true in verse (Baker 1988, 77).

### *References to Singing, Hymns, Music, and Musicians in Charles Wesley's Journal*

The *Journal of the Rev. Charles Wesley, M.A.* An Introduction and Occasional Notes, by Thomas Jackson (2 vols. 1849. Reprint. Grand Rapids, MI: Baker Book House, 1980) covers approximately one half of Charles's career, 1736-56, and focuses primarily on his experiences as preacher/song leader/poet of the revival and an itinerante Anglican priest. The text begins in Frederica, Georgia, March 25, 1736, and concludes in Bristol, November 4, 1756. In spite of its many gaps, sometime for as much as two years, the account reflects the energy and excitement of the early and mid-revival years, revealing Charles as the movement's paradigmatic itinerant preacher, song leader, poet, pastor, mentor, organizer, husband, and father, as well as his brother John's most trusted colleague.

This is apparently the first attempt to study the *Journal* from the exclusive standpoint of music and hymnody. With few exceptions, the excerpts are explicit references to singing, hymn singing, song, music, and musicians. Metaphoric uses of singing and song, e.g., "The Lord put a new song in her mouth" (Oct. 11, 1747), are not included.

Wesley apparently used "praising" and "rejoicing" interchangeably with "singing," i.e., "We accepted it as a challenge to stay, and continued an hour longer, singing and praising God" (Sunday, May 24, 1741); and "rejoicing," "We kept rejoicing till one in the morning"; "For three hours we sang, rejoiced, and gave thanks" (August 25, 1741).

In many instances Wesley includes the full texts as well as excerpts from a number of hymns. These are included where they provide insight to Wesleyan hymnic performance practice or relate to specific events in his ministry. No attempt has been made to provide sources or compare the texts in the *Journal* with other versions in other printings.

The country, village, city, or region are included in brackets preceding the excerpt.

References to prayer and praise, and preaching and singing are often joined, e.g., "Before seven we came to Eltham. . . . We prayed, and sang, and shouted all the way" (Thurs., June 8, 1738).

Charles's strong singing and speaking voice is often mentioned as a defense against those who would disturb his preaching: "A troop poured in from a neighbouring alehouse, and set up their champion, a schoolmaster, upon a bench over against me. For nearly an hour he spake for his master, and I for mine; but my voice prevailed (Mon., Mar. 17, 1740). While field-preaching, Charles could presumably be heard by the multitudes: "At five I took the field again; but such a sight I have rarely seen! Thousands and thousands had been waiting some hours, Protestant and Papists, high and low. . . . I cried after them for an hour, to the utmost extent of my voice, yet without hoarseness or weariness" (Sun.,

Aug. 21, 1748). On several occasions a sore throat prevented his preaching, e.g., Sept. 15, 1749, "My throat grew worse and worse, so that I could not preach in the evening."

Congregational singing is sometimes used to ward off those who attempted to disrupt Methodist worship: "We had a most triumphant watchnight. . . . The enemy did not like our employment, and stirred up his servants . . . but our voices prevailed. We sung the "Hymns in a Tumult" [from *Hymns for Times of Trouble and Persecution*, 1744] with great calmness and consolation" (Fri., Oct. 1, 1756).

Singing often occurs at funerals and graveside and no doubt prompted the writing and use of distinctive Wesleyan hymns on death and dying, e.g., Fri., May 8, 1741, "We solemnized the funeral of our sister Hooper, and rejoiced over her with singing; particularly that hymn which concludes—

> Thus may we all our parting breath
> Into the Saviour's hands resign;
> O, sister, let me die thy death,
> And let thy latter end be mine!

Singing also accompanies Charles's sense of fulfillment, e.g., "I concluded the day and month as I would wish to conclude my life" (July 30, 1744).

Charles's courtship with Sally included social singing with her and with others. "Quite spent with examining the classes, I was much revived in singing with Miss Burdock and Sally" (Tues., June 28, 1748).

Charles's relationships and contacts with noted musicians and patrons of the theater are included, e.g., John F. Lampe and Mrs. Rich, March 29, 1746; and Mrs. Rich and Johann C. Pepusch, April 29, 1748. Nicholas Temperley comments that evangelicals and the Wesleys cultivated a relationship with patrons of the theater in order to gain support for charitable activity:

> There is some apparent irony in the fact that the public
> theatres, generally regarded as a hotbed of prostitution,

and as such condemned by Methodist and Evangelical clergy, were also a prime resource for a charity supported by these same clergy, who sought to alleviate one of prostitution's worst consequences [venereal disease]. A possible explanation is that a number of the patients at the [Lock] hospital may have been members of the theatrical and musical professions, so that their former colleagues felt a special duty to help them (Temperley 1993, 46).

The *Journal* records Charles's abiding witness as a Church of England itinerant priest, particularly his faithful attendance at the sacrament of Holy Communion with recounting the emotions that were shared during the administration of the sacrament. Charles demonstrated his ability to be at home in both a structured liturgical context as well as the revival's improvisational ethos. For example, he cites four times that he either partakes or administered the sacrament at Christ Church, Oxford, and at Kingswood in a ten-day period, August 24 to September 2, 1744.

In some instances he cites the power of the sacrament to move persons to tears, e.g., "All were melted into gracious tears at the sacrament" (London, Jan. 4), and [At Kingswood, Sun., March 31, 1745] "I administered the sacrament to the Society . . . [and] the whole congregation were moved to cry after him." On at least one occasion the sacrament resulted in the opposite, "I gave the sacrament, but without power or life. I had no comfort in it, no singing between, no prayer after it" (Sun., Feb. 3, 1751). On forgiving grace flowing from the sacrament, Charles writes, "In conference, I found one who had received forgiveness in the sacrament" (August 31, 1748). He also administered the sacrament of baptism to a Quaker and a Baptist [rebaptism?] when "all were moved by the descent of that Spirit: many wept, and trembled, and rejoiced. The persons baptized, most of all" (June 2, 1751).

On another occasion the two sacraments were combined, "I baptized a young Quaker at Kingswood; and then we all joined in the Lord's supper. He was mightily present in both sacraments; and afterwards gave me words to shake the soul of those that heard" (June 16, 1751).

It is interesting to note that for his hymn-writing efforts, Charles was awarded a modest stipend of £100 per year from the income of John's publishing activity (Jan., 30, 1748), which became an issue in John Wesley's negotiation of a contract with Mr. Gwynne for the proposed marriage of his daughter Sally to Charles.

### 1736

Thurs., March 25. [Frederica, Georgia] After spending an hour at the camp, in singing Psalms as suited the occasion, I went to bed in the hut, which was thoroughly wet with the day's rain.

### 1737

Tues., October 11. I set out for London. In a mile's riding my horse fell lame. I sung the 91st psalm and put myself under divine protection.

Sun., October 30. [Ironmonger's-Lane] After preaching the same sermon here [as at St. Helen's], we drank tea at Mr. Chadwick's, and then took coach for College-Street. They were much delighted with the singing there, and edified, I hope, by George Whitefield's example. It was near eleven before I left them at their own house.

### 1738

Thurs., January 3. [Blendon] We were joined by Mr. [Henry] Piers [Vicar of Bexley], the Minister of Bexley, who delighted in every opportunity of conversing, singing, and praying with us.

Sat., February 18. I rode over to Stanton-Harcourt to see John and my sister. My brother [John] met us. We prayed and sang together.

Sat., April 8. I got abroad to the evening prayers of Christ-church [Oxford]; and received comfort from the lessons and anthem.

Tues., April 25. Soon after five, as we were met in our little chapel [in Blendon], Mrs. Delamotte came to us. We sang, and fell into a dispute whether conversion was gradual or instantaneous.

Wed., April 26. I passed the day at Mr. Piers's, in singing and reading, and mutual encouragement.

Sat., May 13. [London] At night my brother came, exceeding heavy. I forced him (as he had often forced me) to sing an hymn to Christ; I almost thought He would come while we were singing.

Mon., May 22. [Charles's conversion was on the previous day, Pentecost.] My brother coming, we joined in intercession for him. In the midst of prayer, I almost believed the Holy Ghost was coming upon him. In the evening we sang and prayed again.

Tues., May 23. At nine I began an hymn upon my conversion, but was persuaded to break off, for fear of pride. Mr. [John] Bray [mechanic in Little Britain] coming, encouraged me to proceed in spite of Satan. I prayed Christ to stand by me, and finished the hymn.

Wed., May 24. [The day of John's conversion] I was much pleased to-day at the sight of Mr. Ainsworth, a little child, full of grief, and fears, and love. At our repeating the line of the hymn, "Now descend, and shake the earth," he fell down as in an agony. I found a general delight in their singing, but little attention: yet was not disquieted. We passed the afternoon in prayer, singing, and conference. . . . Towards ten, my brother was brought in triumph by a troop of our friends, and declared, "I believe." We sang the hymn [was the tune CRUCIFIXION TUNE, 706 in *Hymns and Psalms*?] with great joy, and departed with prayer.

Trinity Sunday, May 28. I spent the morning with James Hutton, in prayer, and singing, and rejoicing.

Sat., June 3. In the evening Mr. Brown, Holland, and others called. I was very averse to coming among them, but forced myself to it, and spent two or three hours in singing, reading, and prayer. This exercise a little revived me; and I found myself much assisted to pray.

Mon., June 5. In the afternoon I met Mrs. Sims, with Mr. and Mrs. Burton, at Islington. . . . We rejoiced together in prayer and singing; and left the rest of the company much stirred up to wait for the same unspeakable gift.

Wed., June 7. I went to Mrs. Sims, and passed the afternoon in singing and reading the promises.

Thurs., June 8. Before seven we came to Elthem. . . . We prayed, and sang, and shouted all the way.

Fri., June 9. [Bexley] Mr. Bray relating the inward workings of God upon his soul, and I the great things he had lately done for me, and our friends at London. . . . We walked, and sang, and prayed in the garden.

Sun., June 11. We took coach for church. In singing I observed Hetty join with a mixture of fear and joy. I earnestly prayed, and expected she should meet with something to confirm her in the service. Both the Psalms [sung?] and lessons were full of consolation.

Fri., June 16. After dinner Jack Delamotte came for me. We took coach; and by the way he told me, that when we were last together at Blendon, in singing,

> Who for me, for me hast died,

he found the words sink into his soul; could have sung for ever, being full of delight and joy.

Sat., June 24. [Riding to Blendon] [Delamotte's] objection was, that it was unjust of God to make sinners equal with us, who had laboured perhaps many years. We proposed singing an hymn. He saw the title, "Faith in Christ," and owned he could not bear it.

Mon., June 26. I joined with Mr. Piers in singing,

> Shall I, for fear of feeble man,
> thy Spirit's course in me restrain?

and in hearty prayer for Mrs. Delamotte.

Wed., June 28. I went to Mr. Sims's, in expectation of Christ. Several of our friends were providentially brought thither. We joined in singing and prayer. The last time we prayed, I could not leave off, but was still forced to go on.

Sat., July 1. At Mrs. Claggett's . . . we sang, and rejoiced together, and went to the house of God as friends.

Sun., July 2. At Mr. Sim's . . . [one of the troop] Mrs. Harper . . . received the Spirit, by the hearing of faith; but feared to confess it. We sung the hymn to Christ. At the words "Who for me, for me hath died," she burst out into tears and outcries, "I believe, I believe!" and sunk down. . . . We sang and prayed again.

Mon., July 10. In going to Mr. Chapman's I met Margaret Beutiman, and bade her follow, for we were several of us to join in prayer there. . . . We sang, and pleaded the promises. In the midst of prayer, Margaret received the atonement, and professed her faith without wavering. . . . Mrs. Storer, a sister of Mr. Bray's, complain[ed] of the hardness of her heart. . . . While we were singing the hymn to the Father, she did find the rest she sighed after; was quite pierced, as she said, her heart ready to burst, and her whole nature overpowered.

Sat., July 15. [Newgate] I took coach with Metcalf; preached the threefold state with boldness; gave the sacrament. I went thence to Mrs. Claggett's; sang, rejoiced, and gave thanks, in behalf of both the maids, now added to the church by true divine faith.

Tues., July 18. At night I was locked in [Newgate prison] with Bray in one of the cells. We wrestled in mighty prayer. All the criminals were present; and all delightfully cheerful. The soldier, in particular, found his comfort and joy increase every moment. . . . We sang [Samuel Wesley, Sr.'s],

> Behold the Saviour of mankind,
>   Nail'd to the shameful tree!
> How vast the love that him inclined
>   To bleed and die for thee, & c.

It was one of the most triumphant hours I have ever known. Yet on [*sic.*]

Wed., July 19th, I rose very heavy, and backward to visit them for the last time. At six I prayed and sang with them all together. [At the Tyburn gallows] The Black had spied me coming out of the coach, and saluted me with his looks. As often as his eyes met mine, he smiled with the most composed, delightful countenance I ever way saw. . . . I never saw such calm triumph, such incredible indifference to dying. We sang several hymns; particularly,

> Behold the Saviour of mankind,
> Nail'd to the shameful tree;

and the hymn entitled, "Faith in Christ," which concludes,

> A guilty, weak, and helpless worm,
>   Into thy hands, I fall:
> Be thou my life, my righteousness,
>   My Jesus, and my all.

Sat., Aug. 12. We were warmed by reading George Whitefield's Journal. I walked with Metcalf, &c., in great joy, wishing for a place to sing in, when a blacksmith stopped us. We turned into his house, sang an hymn, and went on our way rejoicing.

Fri., Aug. 18. [Islington] I prayed and rejoiced with [Mrs. Brockmar and company]. We got upon the leads [lead roof covering] and sang; full of zeal, and life, and comfort. I read prayers; and, with Mr. Brockmar and others, returned to singing at Mr. Stonehouse's [vicar at St. Mary's, Islington]. He read us an Homily. At seven we all walked out; were driven by the hard rain to a shed, where we sang and preached to those about us. I came, wet through, to Mr. Bray's: joined our friends there, in singing, reading, and prayer. A young man received faith in that hour.

Sat., Aug. 19. At Mr. Stonehouse's I read prayers with some life. . . . We sang on the leads, as before.

Thurs., Aug. 31. At the society I read my sermon, "The Scripture hath concluded all under sin," and urged upon each my usual question, "Do you deserve to be damned?" Mrs. Platt, with the utmost vehemence, cried out, "Yes; I do, I do!" . . . I asked her, if she believed in Jesus. She answered in full assurance of faith. We sang and rejoiced over her (she still continued kneeling), joined in thanksgiving; but her voice was heard above ours.

Sun., Sept. 24. [After preaching at Islington church] None went out, as they had threatened, and frequently done heretofore; especially the well-dressed hearers, "where'er I mentioned hell to ears polite," and urged that rude question, "Do you deserve to be damned?" We sang, rejoiced, and gave thanks at Mr. Stonehouse's; and again at Mrs. Hankinson's.

Wed., Sept. 27. In our way to Oxford, I talked closely with my fellow-traveler, Mr. Combes. He expressed his desire of faith: I was moved to sing, "Salvation by faith," then "Faith in Christ." . . . We sang and shouted all the way to Oxford.

Mon., Oct. 2. [Oxford] I dined at Mr. Brockmar's; and we admonished one another in psalms and hymns and spiritual songs. I went, with the three Miss Claggetts [and John Wesley], to our poor sick woman.

Sun., Oct. 15. I heard Hutchins at St. Lawrence's: had much comfort and meltings in prayer after the sacrament. I preached the one thing needful at Islington, and added much extempore; sang at Mr. Stonehouse's.

Thurs., Nov. 16. After morning prayers, I baptized Mrs. Bell with hypothetical baptism. I sang and prayed with assistance, at Mr. Stonehouse's.

Tues., Dec. 19. I asked my friend Stonehouse, "Dost thou believe in the Son of God?" And he could confidently answer, "Yet, I do, and now know that I believe." We sang (M. Hankinson joining us) in the spirit of faith, and triumphed in the name of the Lord our God.

Sat., Dec. 23. I was deeply affected in singing at Blendon: retired, and poured out my soul in prayer for love.

### 1739

Mon., Jan. 22. Lady Crisp sent for me. I went, and found Mr. Stonehouse there. She behaved with great courtesy. I transcribed an hymn for Miss. [no last name] After supper, her ladyship spoke largely in praise of marriage. I saw, and pitied, my poor, friend sorely beset. We sang. It was late before we parted.

Fri., Jan. 26. At Dr. Newton's I sang and prayed with them: much affected now; well pleased last night.

Sat., Jan. 27. I carried Bray to Mrs. Whitcomb's; the Claggetts, Metcalf, and his mother, and Hester Hobson were there. We communicated, prayed, and sang with great life and comfort. I slept at Blendon.

Wed., Feb., 14. I read prayer at Newgate [prison], and preached the law first, and then the Gospel. We sang, "Invitation to sinners." All were affected.

Thurs., Feb. 15. [Islington] At the Society I expounded the woman of Samaria. When I had done, she [Miss Crisp's daughter] ran to me, and cried, "I do, I do believe! those words which you spoke came with power, 'Him that cometh unto me, I will in no wise cast out.' An unknown peace flowed with them into my soul." We sang, rejoiced, and gave thanks to the pardoning God in her behalf.

Mon., Feb. 19. I prayed in the prison with Anne Dodd, well-disposed, weary of sin, longing to break loose. I preached powerfully on the last day. I prayed after God for the poor harlots. Our sisters carried away one in triumph. I followed to M. Handon's, who took charge of the returning prodigal. Our hearts were overflowed with pity for her. She seemed confounded, silent, testifying her joy and love by her tears only. We sang and prayed over her in great confidence.

Tues., Feb. 20. I waked full of concern for the poor harlot; and began an hymn for her. At five I called on Miss Crisp; then on Mr. Stonehouse, where I expounded the woman taken in adultery.

Mon., Mar. 12. I was at Newgate with Bray. I prayed, sang, exhorted with great life and vehemence.

Sun., Mar. 25. Betty Hopson came, and prayed that today we might have a feast of fat things. Mr. Stonehouse was full of love, and preached an excellent sermon on faith. After the sacrament we continued our triumph. I preached with power, "Lazarus raised." They sang and prayed at the room. Great was our rejoicing in the Lord.

Tues., Mar. 27. At Mr. Crouch's I expounded on persecution. A man cried out, "That's a lie." We betook ourselves to prayer and singing. The shout of a King was in the midst of us. The man came up quite affable. Another asked what that comfort and joy meant: I calmly invited him to experience it.

Sun., April 1. I preached at St. Catherine's where I met my old friend Mrs. Paine, of East-Grinstead. I administered the sacrament. I dined at Chrissy Anderson's; went in a coach with her and Esther to Islington; comforted in the way while singing. . . . I prayed at Fetterlane, that the Lord might be in the midst of us; received a remarkable answer. B. Howers, in strong pangs, groaned, screamed, roared out. I was not offended by it—nor edified. We sang and praised God with all our might. I could not get home till eleven.

Tues., May 22. Miss Raymond carried me in her coach to Islington. My friend Stonehouse was delighted to see me. We sang together and prayed, as in the months that are past.

Thurs., May 24. I met Miss Raymond (as almost every day,) and joined with her and our friends in prayer and singing.

Sun., May 27. [Broadoaks?] Still Mr. Claggett opposed my preaching. I went to church, where I preached the new birth. We returned singing.

Wed., June 6. Above [more than] sixty of the poor people had passed the night in Mr. Delamotte's barn, singing and rejoicing. I sang and prayed with them before the door.

Thurs., June 7. I was minded to rebuke the famous Prophetess Lavington . . . but I sat quiet and replied not. I offered at last to sing, which she allowed, but did not join.

Mon., June 18. I sang and prayed at Mrs. Euster's, a lively, gracious soul; but too apt to depend on her inward feelings.

Tues., June 19. I felt nothing in my heart but peace. I prayed and sang at Bray's; but some hours after, at West's sank down in great heaviness and discouragement.

Mon., July 3. [Mr. Dean] used his utmost address to bring me off from preaching abroad, from expounding in houses, from singing psalms.

Mon., July 9. I corrected Mr. Cennick's hymns for the press.

Mon., Aug. 20. [Bristol] Mr. Seward's cousin Molly . . . could not pray; could not bear our singing, nor have any rest in her spirit.

Tues., Aug. 21. Our singing in the garden drew two sincere women to us, who sought Christ sorrowing.

Wed., Aug. 22. This morning the work upon poor Robin appeared to be God's work. The words [st. 3: 5-6, "And can it be that I should gain"] that made the first impression were,

> 'Tis mercy all, immense and free,
> For, O my God, it found out me!

Sun., Aug. 26. [Kennington parish] I concluded with singing and invitation to sinners.

Mon., Aug. 27. [In Elby] We prayed and sang alternately, till faith came, God blew with his wind, and the waters flowed.

Sun., Sept. 16. [Hanham-Mount] I lifted up my voice like a trumpet, and in a few minutes drove him [Satan] out of the field [the bowling-green]. For about an hour I preached the Gospel with extraordinary power.

Wed., Oct. 3. [Bath?} Sarah Townsend informed me, that on Sunday evening, while we were singing, "Come to judgment, come away," she found and felt in herself that she *durst* come; the Spirit in that instant sealing her pardon upon her heart.

Fri., Oct. 5. We betook ourselves and let her [Mrs. Granil] pray; for I never heard any pray like her. We laid open the promises, sang, and prayed for her till the Comforter came.

Tues., Oct. 30. [In a letter to the Bishop of Bristol] Jane Connor, at Baptist-Mills, found the power of the Lord present to heal her. Jane Parker experienced the same, while we were singing.

## 1740

Sun., Mar. 16. [Gloucester] An officer from the Mayor met and desired me to come to him. I said I would first wait upon my Lord . . . . I went on. Mr. Henry met me with threats and revilings. I began singing.

> Shall I, for fear of feeble man,
> Thy Spirit's course in me restrain.

I broke out into singing with T. Maxfield, and let them carry me whither they would. At the bridge in the lane they left me. There I stood, out of the liberty of the Corporation, and gave out,

> Angel of God, whate'er betide,
> The summons I obey.

[At the school-house] I spoke convincingly, to some scoffers in particular, who could not long stand it. [Wesley quotes from his doxological stanza]

> Sing ye to our God above
> Praise eternal as his love!

Mon., Mar. 17. [Gloucester?] A troop poured in from a neighbouring alehouse, and set up their champion, a schoolmaster, upon a bench over against me. For nearly an hour he spake for his master, and I for mine; but my voice prevailed. Sometimes we prayed, sometimes sang and gave thanks. . . . In the midst of tumult, reproach, and blasphemy, I enjoyed a sweet calm.

Tues., Mar. 18. While I was concluding [preaching], my friend the schoolmaster set up his throat. We had recourse to singing, which quite spoiled his oration. [After preaching] we spent an hour in songs of triumph. Some Quakers joined us, and found their giving God praises with their lips did not at all obstruct the melody of the heart.

Tues., Mar. 25. [Evesham] I drank tea with one that *was* a sinner, but now looks unto Jesus. I walked out with brother Maxfield to the river-side, and spent a comfortable hour in prayer and singing. . . . I finished Matt. v. with the Society. All was quiet till the last hymn. Then I heard the enemy roaring, and gave out another.

Sun., Mar. 30. [Westcot] In the pulpit I opened the book on, "The Spirit of the Lord is upon me, because the Lord hath anointed me to preach the Gospel to the poor." I described our Lord's prophetic office, and the persons on whom alone he could perform it. We returned from the altar with the voice of praise and thanksgiving, among such as keep holiday. Mrs. M. felt every word we sang.

Good Friday, April 4. I called on a multitude of sinners at the Foundery, "Behold the Lamb of God, which taketh away the sins of the world." . . . I called with Maxfield on Molther in the afternoon. . . . [We] only talked in general against running after ordinances. We parted as we met, without either prayer or singing. The time for these poor exercises is past.

April 6, Easter-day. [In the evening with the bands at Bowers's] . . . without losing an hour in dumb show, I gave out an hymn, and prayed according God. For an hour I spoke freely, no one forbidding. . . . [I told them] to go on to perfection.

Tues., April 8. [At the Foundery] Jane Jackson and others witnessed what God had done for their souls, through our ministry. . . . His

[Christ's] power overshadowed us at this time; therefore our heart danced for joy, and in our song did we praise him.

Fri., April 11. [Wapping] May felt the pangs of the new birth. Behold, a cry, "The Bridegroom cometh!" I knew not when to leave off preaching, praying, singing.

Sun., April 13. I received the sacrament at St. Paul's. [Later] My soul was exceeding sorrowful at the love-feast, and so much dispute . . . . Many bore their testimony to the truth of our doctrine, and that the Moravians, since Peter Böhler, had added nothing to us. In singing and prayer my spirit revived. We praised the Lord with supernatural joy, and magnified his name together.

Wed., April 16. I met the Society at the Foundery; recommended true stillness *in* the use of means; sang, prayed, and exhorted with much freedom and love, till Mr. Simpson declared against the sacrament, and asserted that no unjustified person ought to receive it. . . . After Mr. Simpson had spoke all he had to say, I appeared, and concluded with the hymn on the means of grace.

Tues., April 22. [Islington] At Crouch's Society many were wounded. I left among them the hymn entitled, "The Means of Grace," which I have printed as an antidote to stillness. [The *Journal* editor notes that the poem was later printed as two hymns, "Long have I seem'd to serve thee, Lord" and "Still for thy lovingkindness, Lord."]

I attended my brother to Fetter-Lane. The first hour passed in dumb show, as usual; the next in trifles not worth naming. John Bray, who seems to be a pillar, if not the main one, expelled one brother, and reproved me from not attending my band. We parted as we met with little of singing, less of prayer, and nothing of love. However, they carried their point, which was to divert my brother from speaking.

Ascension-day [Tuesday], May 15. [At the Society] Sarah Church informed me she had received forgiveness the night Mr. Simpson expounded at Rag-fair; not under his preaching, which was quite dead to her, but in singing an hymn which I gave out. So did Anne Roberts, after hearing the work, in the same carnal ordinance of singing.

Mon., June 2. [London; after preaching] I talked with several in whom the work of conversion is effectually begun [including] . . . Mary Peck, whom God showed her heart in singing.

Sun., July 13. [Bristol] I preached at Rose Green on the fall of man. (Gen. iii.) . . . We walked over the waste to the school, singing and rejoicing. It was their love-feast. Two hundred were assembled in the Spirit of Jesus.

Sun., July 27. I preached the Gospel in Kingswood with double power, from Isai. xl.: "Comfort ye, comfort ye my people, saith your God. . . . Before sermon, I declared our brother Cennick's entire agreement with me in the belief of universal redemption; and he confirmed my saying with an hymn of his own. Never did I find my spirit more knit to him.

Wed., Aug. 6. [Bristol] In great heaviness I spoke to the women-bands, as taking my farewell: sang the hymn which begins

> While sickness shakes the house of clay,
>     And, sapp'd by pain's continued course,
> My nature hastens to decay,
>     And waits the fever's friendly force.

After speaking a few faint words to the brethren, I was immediately taken with a shivering; and then the fever came.

Wed., Oct. 8. I was much revived by the sight of Margaret Thomas, dying in the highest triumph of faith. I could not help asking,

> Is this the soul so late weigh'd down
>     By cares and sins, by griefs and pains?
> Whither are all thy terrors gone?
>     Jesus for thee the victory gains,
> And death, and sin, and Satan yield
> To faith's unconquerable shield.

Thurs., Oct. 23. [Bristol] I met several of the bands at the house of our departed sister Purnell, and solemnly rejoiced over her, with singing.

Tues., Oct. 28. We sang a funeral hymn over him [Mr. Seward], and were comforted in the hope of soon meeting him again, where no sower of tares, no reprobating Pharisee, shall ever part us more.

Sat., Nov. 8. [Cardiff] I spent the day in singing and close confer- ence, with some who would fain persuade themselves they had faith, without forgiveness.

Tues., Nov. 17. [London] I preached at St. Bride's . . . . We were set- ting out from the public-house, when God brought Howell Harris to us.

All misunderstandings vanished at sight of each other. . . . We sang an hymn of triumph.

While we were talking [they] made another attempt to break in, and get at me . . . they went; and we continued our triumph in the name of the Lord our God. The shout of the King was among us. We sang on unconcerned, though those sons of Belial, the players, had beset the house. . . . We prayed and sang with great tranquillity till one in the morning.

Wed., Nov. 19. [I] preached the pure Gospel from the woman of Canaan. . . . Some of the greatest opposers wept, especially a young lady, for whose entertainment the players had acted me, sang, and prayed, and trembled exceedingly.

## 1741 (The Journal begins with April 20 )

Mon., April 20. [Downing] We prayed and sung alternately for two hours; and the Lord, we trust, enlarged and established our hearts.

Tues., April 21. I hastened to the joyful funeral of our sister [Hannah Richardson]. . . . The whole society followed her to her grave. Through all the city Satan raged exceedingly in his children, who threw dirt and stones at us. . . . After the funeral we joined in the following hymn [Stanza 1 included here]:

> Come, let us who in Christ believe,
>    With saints and angels join,
> Glory, and praise, and blessing give,
>    And thanks to grace divine.

Sat., April 25. [Kingswood] Our thanksgiving-notes multiply more and more. One wrote thus:—"There was not a word came out of your mouth last night, but I could apply it to my own soul, and witness it the doctrine of Christ.

> 'O for a thousand tongues to sing
> My dear Redeemer's praise!'"

Fri., May 8. [Kingswood] We solemnized the funeral of our sister Hooper, and rejoiced over her with singing; particularly that hymn which concludes.—

> Thus may we all our parting breath
>    Into the Saviour's hands resign;
> O, sister, let me die thy death,
>    And let thy latter end be mine!

My text was, "Lord, now lettest thou thy servant depart in peace." A great multitude attended her to her grave. There we sang another hymn of triumph.

Whitsunday, May 17. The fire was kindled while we were singing,

> Bear we witness unto Thee,
>    Thou thy light to all dost give,
> That the world through it may see
>    Their Saviour, and believe.

Mon., May 18. A poor soldier confessed to me, that God had opened his eyes to see his universal love: I was repeating that verse,—

> Arise, O God, arise,
>   Thy glorious cause maintain;
> Hold forth the bloody sacrifice,
>   For every sinner slain.

Sun., May 24. [Bristol] I heard my brother at the Mills, and attended him to the Society. We had the cloud [disturbers] in our assembly. . . . One of his [Satan's] subjects threw a stone into the room, which had no permission to hurt. We accepted it as a challenge to stay, and continued an hour longer, singing and praising God.

Sun., June 28. A day much to be remembered. . . . Last night Howel Harris told me he would come to our Society. I bade him come in God's name. We were singing,

> Thee triumphantly we praise,
>   Vie with all thy hosts above;
> Shout thine universal grace,
>   Thine everlasting love;

when W. Hooper, by my order, brought him. I prayed according to God; gave out an hymn which we might all join in. . . . I asked Howel whether he had a mind to speak [and] for half an hour . . . [he] gave an account of his conversion by *irresistible grace* mixing with his experience the impossibility of falling, God's unchangeableness, &c. [The assembly was asked if I should allow him to continue.] Again they forbade me in strong words; upon which I gave out,

> Break forth into joy,
> Your Comforter sing, &c.

They did break forth as the voice of many waters, or mighty thunderings. . . . Howel Harris would have entered into the dispute, but . . . I cut off the sentence of reprobation which I foresaw coming, with,

> Praise God, from whom pure blessings flow,
> Whose bowels yearn on *all* below;
> Who would not have one sinner lost;
> Praise Father, Son, and Holy Ghost.

Tues., July 14. [Cardiff] I reached in the afternoon to the prisoners, "How shall I give thee up, O Ephraim?" Above twenty were felons. The word melted them down. Many tears were shed at the singing that, [st. 4:1 "Where shall my wondering soul begin"] Outcasts of men to you I call, &c.

Fri., July 17. [The Castle, Cardiff] The voice praise and thanksgiving was heard in this dwelling-place. Before, at, and after supper we sang, and blessed God with joyful lips. Those in the parlour and kitchen were continually honouring, by offering him praise. I thought it looked like the house of faithful Abraham. We called our brethren of Kingswood to be present with us in spirit, and continued rejoicing with them till morning.

Sun., Aug. 2. [Kingswood] I preached a funeral sermon over our sister Rachel Peacock, who died in the Lord most triumphantly. She had had continual joy in the Lord, which made her cry out "Though I groan, I feel no pain at all: Christ so rejoices and fills my heart." Her mouth also was filled with laughter, and her tongue with joy. She sang hymns incessantly. "Christ," said she, "is in my heart, and one minute with the Lord is worth a million of ages."

Thurs., Aug. 6. Coming to pray by a poor Welshwoman . . . I sat and heard her sing the new song, until even my hard heart was melted.

Tues., Aug. 25. [Cardiff] For three hours we sang, rejoiced, and gave thanks; then rode to Porthkerry, where I read prayers, and discoursed near two hours on the pool of Bethesda. The whole congregation were in tears.

Thurs., Aug. 27. I went to a revel at Lanvane. . . . An old dancer of threescore fell down under the stroke of the hammer. She could never be convinced before that there was any harm in those innocent pleasures.

Fri., Aug. 28. I preached again in Porthkerry church. . . . At six I expounded Isai. liii. in the court-yard. . . . I spent the evening in conference with those who desired to be on the Society . . . . I sang and prayed with them till ten; with the family till midnight.

Sun., Sept. 13. I preached at Cardiff, then at Wenvo; the third time at Porthkerry, and the last at Fonmon. The remainder of the night we passed admonishing one another in psalms, and hymns and spiritual songs.

Mon., Sept. 14. We sang on till two; then I rode to a revel at Dennis-Powis.

Wed. Sept. 16. I kept a watchnight at Fonmon, and expounded the ten virgins. We continued singing and rejoicing till two in the morning. O that the world were partakers with us!

### The *Journal* has no entries from September 22, 1741, to January 2, 1743.

Sat., May 21. [Wednesbury] I spent the morning in conference with several who have received the atonement under my brother, &c. I saw a piece of ground given us by a dissenter to build a preaching-house upon, and consecrated it by an hymn. I walked with many of the brethren to Walsal, singing.

Wed., May 25. [Sheffield] At six I went to the Society-house, next door to our brother Bennet's. Hell from beneath was moved to oppose us. As soon as I was in the desk with David Taylor, the floods began to lift up their voice. An officer (Ensign Garden) contradicted and blasphemed. I took no notice of him, and sung on. The stones flew thick, hitting the desk and people.

Mon., May 30. Near Ripley my horse threw, and fell upon, me. My companion thought I had broke my neck; but my leg only was bruised, my hand sprained, and my head stunned; which spoiled my making hymns, or thinking at all, till the next day; when the lord brought safe to Newcastle.

Sat., June 4. [Pelton] To-day, one who came from the alehouse, drunk, was pleased to fall into a fit for my entertainment, and beat himself heartily. I thought it a pity to hinder him; so instead of singing over him, as had been often done, we left him to recover at his leisure. . . .

Last night, before I began, I gave public notice, that whosoever cried so as to drown my voice, should, without any man's hurting or judging them, be gently carried to the farthest corner of the room.

Sun., July 24. [Wednock, Cornwall] The Society came. Our hearts danced for joy, and in our song did we praise him.

Sat., July 30. [St. Just] I walked with our brother Shepherd to the Land's-end, and sang, on the extremist point of the rocks [first stanza included here],

> Come, Divine Immanuel, come,
> Take possession of thy home;
> Now thy mercy's wings expand,
> Stretch throughout the happy land.

Tues., Oct. 25. [Walsale] The accusers mentioned the only crime against [me]. . . . He makes people rise at five in the morning to sing psalms. . . . Never was I before in so primitive an assembly. We sang praises lustily, and with good courage. . . . We laid us down and slept, and rose up again; for the Lord sustained us. We assembled before day to sing hymns to Christ as God.

## 1744

Fri., Feb. 3. The poor people from Darlaston are the greatest sufferers. . . . And still if they hear any of them singing or reading the Scripture, they force open their doors by day and by night, and spoil and beat them with all impurity.

Sat., Feb. 18 [From J. Healey in Nottingham] I heard of a remarkable providence. A poor drunkard . . . was moved . . . [to] come to the preaching; by which he escaped being crushed to death by the fall of his house. . . . Just before it fell, his wife took one with her to the window, to sing an hymn, and so escaped.

Sun., March 14. [At Leeds] in an old upper-room. . . . After singing, I shifted my place, to draw them to the upper end. . . . I moved again. . . .

In that instant the floor sank. . . . I cried out, "Fear not, the Lord is with us; our lives are all safe!" and then,—

Praise God, from whom all blessings flow.

Thurs., March 15. [In Wakefield, before Justice Burton to answer charges of praying for the Pretender] I answered, "The very reverse is true. We constantly pray for His majesty King George by name. These are such hymns as we sing in our Societies, a sermon I preached before the University. . . ." Here gave them our books, and was bold to say, "I am as true a Church-of-England man, and as loyal a subject as any man in the kingdom."

Half hour after seven we set out for Birstal, and a joyful journey we had. Our brethren met us on the road, and we gathered together on the hill, and sang praises lustily, with a good courage. . . . They begun pulling down John Nelson's house, when our singing damped and put them to flight.

Thurs., July 19. [St. Ives; at John Nance's house] I got an hour by myself in the garden, and was suffered to feel our great weakness. Without were fightings, within fears; but my fears were all scattered by the sight of my dear brethren and children. I rejoiced over them with singing; but their joy and love exceeded. We all rejoiced in hope of meeting Him in the air.

Tues., July 31. [St. Just] I preached in the afternoon to a larger congregation than ever. . . . I walked to the Society; stood upon the hill, and sang, and prayed, and rejoiced with exceeding great joy.

Tues., Aug. 14. [Cardiff] We sang a song of victory for our deceased friend; then went to the house, and rejoiced, and gave thanks; and rejoiced again with singing over him. The spirit, at its departure, had left marks of its happiness on the clay. No sight upon earth, in my eyes, is half so lovely.

Thurs., Aug. 23. I went to Christ-Church [Oxford] prayers, with several of the brethren, who thought it strange to see men in surplices talking, laughing, and pointing, as in a play-house, the whole time of service. [After conference with my brother John] . . . we found the spirit which had drawn us formerly in this place. I preached to a multitude of the brethren, gownsmen, and gentry from the races, who filled our inn and yard. The stranger that intermeddled not with our joy seemed struck and astonished with it, while we admonished one another in psalms, and hymns, &c. O that all the world had a taste for our diversion!

Fri., Nov. 30. [Newcastle] In the evening the waves [the disturbers] so lifted up their voice, that we could only sing for half an hour. The most violent of the rioters had been two of our own Society.

Mon., Dec. 17. [Epworth; the *Journal* editor indicates this hymn was written on the occasion of great adversity. The first stanza is included here.]

> O my Galilean King,
>     Can I glory in this shame?
> Can I this dishonour bring
>     As a suffering for thy Name?

## 1745

Sun., Jan. 27. [London] I paid my last visit to our poor unstable brother Cowper. . . . I buried a sister, who departed in the Lord. I called the multitude at the Foundery, "Come, for all things are now ready." I met the bands; and a solemn, mournful assembly it was. I could speak, sing, pray for nothing but death. We mixed our tears and souls together in that love which death cannot violate.

Fri., May 31. [Islington] We kept a watchnight. Dear Howel Harris I carried into the desk, and we sang together, and shouted for joy, till morning.

Sun., June 23. I had just time to reach Conham chapel by two. . . . While I was speaking of our Lord's appearing, we here alarmed with the loudest clap of thunder I ever heard. . . . Most of the congregation shrieked out, as if the day of the Lord were come. A thought darted into my heart as quick as the lightning, "What if it should be the day of judgment?" I was filled immediately with faith, stronger than death, and rejoiced in hope of the glory of God. The same spirit rested on all the faithful, while I broke out into singing,—

> So shall the Lord the Saviour come,
>   And lightnings round his chariot play:
> Ye lightnings, fly to make him room,
>   Ye glorious storms, prepare his way!

Sat., Aug. 10. [At Shepton-Mallet after I fell] Mr. P. sent me a kind message, and his bath-chair to bring me to his house. I thanked him, but declined his offer, on account of my pain, which unfitted me for any company, except that of my best friends,—the poor. With these I continued praying, singing, and rejoicing for two hours. . . . When my strength was exhausted, they laid me on their bed, the best they had; but I could not sleep for pain.

Tues., Aug. 13. [On Captain Philip's vessel] We spent the day in singing and reading; and by six on Thursday morning, August 15th, landed at Cardiff.

Sat., Oct. 26. [London] I dined at Mrs. R's [the actress, a convert to Methodism whose husband was a proprietor of Covent-garden theatre]. Mr. R [ich] behaved with great civility. I foresee the storm my visit will bring upon him.

### 1746

Thurs., Feb. 6. We sang that hymn [Lampe's setting? See pages 105-10] over her [sister Webb's] corpse, "Ah, lovely appearance of death," and shed a few tears of joy and envy. [See also the account of John Wesley singing the hymn in Dublin, page 109]

Good-Friday, Mar. 28. I drank tea at my sister Wright's, with Mrs. Rich and her two youngest daughters; one the greatest miracles of all accomplishment, both of mind and body, that I have ever seen.

Sat., Mar. 29. I passed the afternoon at Mrs. Rich's, where we caught a Physician [a healing spirit] by the ear, through the help of Mr. Lampe and some of our sisters. This is the true use of music.

Fri., May 2. I rode back to Bristol, and was met with the news of our victory in Scotland. I spoke at night on the first words that presented, "He that glorieth, let him glory in the Lord." We rejoiced unto him with reverence, and thankfully observed the remarkable answer of that petition,

> All their strength o'erturn, o'erthrow,
>   Snap their spears, and break their swords,
> Let the daring rebels know
>   The battle is the Lord's!

Fri., July 25. [Trewallard] I had left my Hymn-book [which collection?] in my chamber, and stepped up for it. . . . [After hearing of a warrant for my arrest] . . . I received strength to preach again in the courtyard, on "Saul, Saul, why persecutest thou me?" The two-edged sword did great execution. I concluded with that hymn,__

> Glory and thanks and praise
>   To Him that hath the key!
> Jesus, they sovereign grace
>   Gives us the victory;
> Baffles the world and Satan's power,
> And open throws the Gospel-door, &c.

Mon., Aug. 11. [Gwennaap] I expressed the gratitude of my heart [for the Spirit's infusion in the Society] in the following thanksgiving:—

> All thanks be to God,
> Who scatters abroad,
> Throughout every place,
> By the least of his servants, his savour of grace:
> Who the victory gave,
> The praise let him have,
> For the work He hath done;
> All honour and glory to Jesus alone! &c

Sun., Aug. 24. [St. Ginnys] Samuel [Trembath] departed in full triumph. His last words were,

> Ready wing'd for their flight
> To the regions of light,
> The horsemen are come,
> The chariots of Israel, to carry me home!

Mon., Oct. 13. I dined at Studley [near Newcastle], where some poor drunkards, offended at our singing, endeavoured a while to silence us; but we fairly outsung them.

## 1747

Sun., Jan. 18. [Leeds] In the midst of my discourse, we all broke out into joy and singing.

Wed., Feb. 25. [Bristol, after overcoming a great disturbance] We joined in hearty praises to our Deliverer, singing the hymn [from *Redemption Hymns*, 1747], Worship, and thanks and blessing, &c.

Mon., April 27. That I might abstain from all appearance of evil, particularly of pride and resentment, I took up my cross, and went in Mrs. Rich's coach to Chelsea. I passed an hour or two at Lampe's before I waited upon one who was once my friend. The first that greeted me was faithful Mrs. M., with her *old professions*; next, Mrs. E.; and last, *that person*; at whose desire I sang, prayed, dined, exhorted, talked of the times, and took my leave.

Wed., Aug. 5. I met the bands in Bristol; and the power of God broke in upon us wonderfully.

Thurs., Aug. 6. I found it again in singing with Miss Wells, Miss Burdock, and eight of our Preachers.

Sun., Oct. 11. [Dublin] I began preaching with great reluctance, at Marybone-lane, where the Spirit came pouring down like a flood. All present were in tears, either of sorrow or joy. We continued above an hour, singing and crying. A more refreshing time I have not known, since I left England.

## 1748

Mon., Feb. 8. Took horse for Tryil's-pass. We overtook a lad whistling one of our tunes. He was a constant hearer, though a Roman, and joined with us in several hymns which he had by heart.

Wed., Feb. 10. At eight I took horse for Athlone. Some overtook us, running in great haste, and one horseman, riding full speed. We suspected nothing and rode on singing, till within half a mile of the town. . . . [After we had been stoned] we halted, and sang a song of triumph and praise to God, who giveth us the victory through our Lord Jesus Christ.

Sun., Feb. 14. At Philip's-town I expounded the prodigal son. About forty dragoons joined me in singing and conference, both before and after. These are all turned from darkness to light, that they may receive forgiveness.

Fri., April 29. [London] Mrs. Rich carried me [in her coach] to Dr. [Johann C.] Pepusch, whose music entertained us much, and his conversation more.

Tues., June 28. [Bristol] Quite spent with examining the classes, I was much revived in singing with Miss Burdock and Sally.

Fri., July 29. [After preaching during a disturbance] I ran with fresh strength to the shell of our room, and continued preaching, singing, rejoicing till midnight.

Sun., Aug. 21. [Christ-church, Cork] I advised them [the crowd of thousands] to go to their several places of worship, and went myself to Christ-church. It is the largest church in Cork, yet quite full. The communion kept us till near ten.

At five I took the field [the marsh] again; but such a sight I have rarely seen! Thousands and thousands had been waiting some hours, Protestant and Papists, high and low . . . cried [preached and sang?] after them for an hour, to the utmost extent of my voice, yet without hoarseness or weariness.

Mon., Sept. 5. On the road [to Bandon] I made the following hymn, for the Roman Catholics in Ireland;— [the first stanza included here]

> Shepherd of souls, the great, the good,
>   Thy helpless sheep behold,
> Those other sheep dispersed abroad,
>   Who are not of this fold.
> By Satan and his factors bound
>   In ignorance and sin,
> Recall them through the Gospel sound,
>   And bring the outcasts in.

Wed., Sept. 7. [Bandon] I spent an hour in the town-hall with some hundreds of them, in prayer and singing.

Sun., Sept. 25. [Athlone] In the evening preaching the great blessing came. Cries of the wounded spirits cannot be described. The place rung with loud calls for "mercy, mercy!" I concluded, and began again, and again; then sung, and prayed, and sung, not knowing how to give over.

Fri., Oct. 7. [Dublin?] I met at Mr. Lunell's, an old Dutch Quaker, who seemed to have deep experience of the things of God. At two Mr. Lampe and his wife called, and were overjoyed to see me. I cannot yet give up my hope, that they are designed for better things than feeding swine; that is, entertaining the gay world.

Mon., Oct. 10. [Enroute to Wales] I blessed God that I did not stay in the vessel [during the storm] last night. A more tempestuous one I do not remember. I wrote a thanksgiving hymn:— [stanza 1 included here]

> All thanks to the Lord,
>   Who rules with a word
> Th' untractable sea,
> And limits its rage by his steadfast decree;
>   Whose providence binds
>   Or releases the winds,
>   And compels them again
> At his beck to put on the invisible chain.

Fri., Dec. 2. By nine I found them at Garth, singing, and was most affectionately received by all, especially Mrs. [Gwynne, Sally's mother].

Fri., Dec. 30. [London] I met Mr. Blackwell with my brother, who proposes £100 a year to be paid me out of the books.

Sat., Dec. 31. I rejoiced to hear of our brother White's translation [death]. I described it in the following hymn:— [Stanza 1 included here]

> O what a soul-transporting sight
>   Mine eyes to-day have seen,
> A spectacle of strange delight
>   To angels and to men!

### 1749

Sat., April 8. [At the wedding of Sally and Charles in Garth] Mr. Gwynne gave her to me (under God): my brother joined our hands. It was a most solemn season of love! Never had I more of the divine presence at the sacrament.

My brother gave out the following hymn:— [Stanza 1 included here]

> Come, thou everlasting Lord,
> By our trembling hearts adored;
> Come, thou heaven-descended Guest,
> Bidden to the marriage-feast!

Fri., June 2. [Hereford] At half-hour past three my beloved Sally, with Mrs. Gwynne and her sister Peg, found me at the Falcon. We sang, rejoiced, and gave thanks till Mr. and Mrs. Hervey came. After dinner we drank tea at their house, and went to see the cathedral.

Sun., Sept. 3. [Kingswood] I rose with my partner [Sally] at four. Both under the word and among the select band, we were constrained to cry after Jesus with mighty prayers and tears. We sang this hymn in my family:— [Stanza 1 included here]

> God of faithful Abraham, hear
> His feeble son and thine,
> In thy glorious power appear,
> And bless my just design:
> Lo! I come to serve thy will,
> All thy blessed will to prove;
> Fired with patriarchal zeal,
> And pure primeval love.

Fri., Sept. 15. My throat grew worse and worse, so that I could not preach in the evening.

Wed., Oct. 25. Among my hearers to-day at Bath, were a son of Lord Chief Justice Lee, my old schoolfellow, Sir Danvers Osborn, and Lord Halifax. They behaved decently, and were particularly taken with the singing.

### 1750

Tues., Feb. 14. [Freshford] An old lady of four-score received me into her house. We spent the time in prayer and singing.

Wed., May 30. [London?] We had a long day's journey to St. Anne's. It was past nine before we got under shelter. Mrs. Rich was there, who, with our old friends, received us gladly.

Thurs., June 21. I took horse at three, and *waked* them [not personified] at Westerham. I passed the day with them in the gardens, reading, singing, and conversing.

## 1751

Sun., Feb. 3. I gave the sacrament, but without power or life. I had no comfort in it, no singing between, no prayer after it.

Tues., April 9. [London] I spent a week with M. Colvil, and Miss Degge, chiefly in reading, singing, and prayer.

Sat., April 13. I passed the evening with Sally at Mr. Ianson's and saw the Prince's funeral pass. [Frederick Louis, son of George II and Prince of Wales, 1707-51] The house was full of strangers. We joined in many suitable hymns, till near midnight.

Mon., May 6. Mr. Lloyd paid us a visit. We passed our time no less useful than agreeably, in reading and singing. He and I witnessed to Mrs. C.'s will.

Fri., May 10. [The first mention in the *Journal* of Charles's home on Charles Street in Bristol] I came safe with Sally to Charles Street. Our friends Vigor, Davis, &c., were there to welcome us. We were much drawn out in prayer.

Tues., May 28. My very good old friend M. Cradock came to see me, with Mrs. Motte. We sang, and conversed, and prayed (particularly for their Lady) as in the former days.

Mon., June 3. My wife accepted her ladyship's invitation, and went with me to see her. We employed an hour or two in very useful conversation, and singing, and prayer.

Tues., June 4. [While I was preaching] He [Mr. Hall] came up toward the desk. Mr. Hamilton stopped him. I gave out an hymn. He sang louder than us all. I spoke sharply of his apostasy, and prayed earnestly for him.

Sat., July 6. We were hardly met, when the sons of Belial poured in upon us, some with their faces blacked, some without shirts, all in rags.

They began to "stand up for the Church," by cursing and swearing, by singing and talking lewdly, and throwing dust and dirt all over us.

Mon., July 8. [Tipton-Green] In the afternoon the Curate met me; a well-disposed youth, just come from College; there his Tutor, Mr. Bentham, gave him an early prejudice for true religion. He invited me to his lodgings, joined with us in serious conversation and singing, and seemed ready for all good impressions.

*[There is no Journal for 1752. There were no entries on music and hymns for 1753.]*

*The Journal for 1754 begins on July 8.*

Wed., July 31. [Norwich, while preaching to about two hundred] A gentleman on horseback gnashed upon me with his teeth; but my voice prevailed, and they retreated to their strong hold, the alehouse. There with difficulty they procured some butchers to appear in their quarrel; yet they had no commission to approach till I had done. Then in the last hymn they made up to the table with great fury. The foremost often lifted up his stick to strike me, being within his reach; but he was not permitted. I stayed to pray for them, and walked quietly to my lodgings. . . . I slept in peace.

Sun., August 4. I met the Society at five, with some new members, or rather candidates. . . . We had sweet fellowship in singing and prayer. . . . I met the Society again after dinner. . . . A few ragged drunkards stood at a distance, but were not suffered to make a noise until I had done. Then they lifted up their voice, which made me begin again. I exhorted, sang, prayed, and exhorted again. . . . Our house was crowded afterwards. For an hour I spoke, sang, prayed after God.

**[The *Journal* has no record from August 14, 1754 to September 1756.]**

Fri., Oct. 1. [York] We had a most triumphant watchnight. . . . The enemy did not like our employment, and stirred up his servants . . . but our voices prevailed. We sung the "Hymns in a Tumult" [from *Hymns for Times of Trouble and Persecution*, 1744] with great calmness and consolation.

Sat., Oct. 2. The whole day was spent in singing, conference, and prayer. I attended the choir [choral evensong] service. The people there were marvelously civil, and obliged me with the anthem I desired, Hab. iii., "a feast for a King," as Queen Anne called it.

Mon., Oct. 11. [Leeds; George Whitefield preached in the watch-night service] They forced me to preach first. . . . My brother George seconded me in the words of our Lord: "I say unto all, Watch." The prayers and hymn were all attended with a solemn power.

Fri., Oct. 22. [Manchester] I began in the evening to expound the whole armour of God, Eph. vi. After I had done, the famous Mr. Ball lifted up his voice; and a magnificent voice it was.

Fri., Oct. 29. [Leeds] The enemy has had a particular grudge to this Society. His first messenger to them was a *still sister*, who abounded in visions and revelations. She came to them as in the name of the Lord, and forbade them to pray, sing, or *go to church*.

### Charles Wesley, *Poet of Lyrical Theology*

We turn to a consideration of Charles Wesley's hymns as the lyrical expression of Wesleyan theology, a unique contribution of the Methodist revival that Thomas A. Langford has described as

> theology-as-hymn, that is, it is theology expressed by, limited by, enlivened by its hymn form. Charles Wesley's theology is "a theology one can sing." In this sense it is a theology with which one can praise; it is a theology with which one can pray, a theology with which one can teach; it is a theology which one can use to initiate, to guide, and to envision the final hope of Christ's existence (Kimbrough 1992, 97).

Langford's description has been extended in Teresa Berger's recent study *Theology in Hymns?* as she concludes that Wesleyan hymns, particularly those included in the 1780 *Collection*, and the singing practice of Methodists, uniquely join doxology speech and theological reflection (Berger 1994, 220).

The vastness and variety of Charles's lyrical output are seen in the great number of his hymns that were selected and edited by John Wesley for inclusion in his definitive 1780 *Collection* and spread throughout its contents reflecting the theology of Methodism and the various activities and interests of its societies.

PART 1
Containing Introductory Hymns

| | | |
|---|---|---|
| Sect. | I. | Exhorting and beseeching to return to God |
| | II. | Describing, 1. The pleasantness of Religion |
| | | 2. The goodness of God |
| | | 3. Death |
| | | 4. Judgment |
| | | 5. Heaven |
| | | 6. Hell |
| | III. | Prayer for a Blessing |

PART II

| | | |
|---|---|---|
| Sect. | I. | Describing   formal Religion |
| | II. | inward Religion |

PART III

| | | |
|---|---|---|
| Sect. | I. | Praying for Repentance |
| | II. | For Mourners convinced of Sin |
| | III. | Brought to the Birth |
| | IV. | Convinced of Backsliding |
| | V. | Recovered |

PART IV

| Sect. | I. | For Believers | Rejoicing |
|---|---|---|---|
| | II. | | Fighting |
| | III. | | Praying |
| | IV. | | Watching |
| | V. | | Working |
| | VI. | | Suffering |
| | VII. | | Groaning for full Redemption |
| | VIII. | | Brought to the Birth |
| | IX. | | Saved |
| | X. | | Interceding for the World |

PART V

| Sect. | I. | For the Society, | Meeting |
|---|---|---|---|
| | II. | | Giving Thanks |
| | III. | | Praying |
| | IV. | | Parting |

### *Charles Wesley's Conversion Hymn*

Methodism's music of the heart—lyrical theology—proceeds from the conversion of Charles Wesley, May 21, 1738. Two years previous he had returned dejected from a no-win task as a short-term missionary in the Georgia colony, March 9 to July 26, 1736, where he served as secretary to the celebrated British prison reformer James Oglethorpe.

Frederick Gill has commented that after Charles returned to London he came under the influence of three persons: William Law, author of *A Serious Call*, whose advice was "Renounce yourself, and be not impatient"; Count Zinzendorf, the Herrnhut Moravian, in whom Charles confided; and Peter Böhler, a young Moravian missionary to whom Charles taught English. During this time Charles also experienced long periods of intense uncertainty, depression, and despair followed by glimmers of hope:

Charles never trod an even course like his more predictable brother. He was either on the heights or in the depths. He was more deeply moved than John, more perceptive, more compassionate. . . . He was of the stuff of which, not heroes, but artists and mystics are made, of the company of Pascal, George Herbert and William Blake (Gill 1964, 67).

Charles's struggle climaxed on Whit [Pentecost] Sunday, May 21, 1738, when, as he relates in his *Journal* 1:92:

I now found myself at peace with God, and rejoiced in hope of loving Christ. My temper for the rest of the day was, mistrust of my own great, but before unknown, weakness. I saw that by faith I stood; by the continual support of faith, which kept me from falling, though of myself I am ever sinking into sin. I went to bed still sensible of my own weakness (I humbly hope to be more and more so) yet confident of Christ's protection.

He also relates that he had begun to write a hymn at his conversion:

Towards ten, my brother was brought in triumph by a troop of our friends, and declared, "I believe." We sang the hymn [to the tune: "Crucifixion Tune," 706 in *Hymns and Psalms*?] with great joy, and departed with prayer (Baker 1962, 3).

While it was not his first poem since "he was already . . . a matured poet" (Baker 1962, xii), it was his very first evangelical hymn. The hymn that was shared at his brother's conversion was probably "Where shall my wondering soul begin" (**342**), and it opens with three stanzas that are the poet's responses for being "redeemed from death and sin"; some are one affirmation:

> That I, a child of wrath and hell,
> I shall be called a child of God!

Others are questions, such as:

> Shall I, the hallowed cross to shun,
> Refuse his righteousness to impart,
> by hiding it within my heart?

That question became a primary goal of the Wesleyan revival: literally telling everyone who would listen the good news of their redemption in Christ. The balance of the hymn is a call to all to believe that "for you the Prince of Glory died," and "Believe, and all your guilt's forgiven."

Line five of stanza two is crucial in understanding the foundation of the Wesleyan revival—knowing and feeling, mind and heart,

> Should know, should feel my sins forgiven
> blest with this antepast of heaven!

—*knowing*, that is, assured of, and *feeling* one's sins forgiven, a foretaste of heaven, as Fanny Crosby would sing it a century later.

Note the bold metaphors in the invitation in stanza four:

> Outcast of men, to you I call,
>     harlots and publicans and thieves;
> he spreads his arms to embrace you all,
>     sinners alone his grace receives.
> No need of him the righteous have;
> he came the lost to seek and save.

This invitation is also echoed in "Glory to God, and praise and love" **(58)**, composed for the first anniversary of his conversion.

"Where shall my wondering soul begin" entered USA Methodist hymnals in 1836, was dropped in 1849, and restored in 1966. *The United Methodist Hymnal* omits stanzas four and six:

> No—tho' the Ancient Dragon rage
>     And call forth all his Hosts to War,
> Tho' Earth's self-righteous Sons engage;
>     Them, and their God alike I dare:

> Jesus the Sinner's Friend proclaim,
> Jesus, to Sinners still the same.
>
> Come all ye *Magdalens* in Lust,
>    Ye Ruffians fell in Murders old;
> Repent, and live: despair and trust!
>    Jesus for you to Death was sold;
> Tho' Hell protest, and Earth repine,
> He died for Crimes like Yours—and mine.

The hymn is one of a trilogy of Charles Wesley's early spiritual-autobiographical hymns in 88.88.88, which also includes "And can it be that I should gain" (**363**) and "Come, O thou traveler unknown" (**386, 387**), "bringing to moving expression the rapture of the soul in its response to the wonder and love of God as proclaimed in the gospel" (Kimbrough 1993).

### *The Wesleyan Doctrine of Grace in Charles Wesley's Hymns*

The foundation of Wesleyan teaching of the new life in Christ is in the three-fold doctrine of grace: prevenient, justifying, sanctifying and perfecting.

Prevenient Grace. God's gifts to the human family, including life, worth, right and wrong, obedience; air, water, light, food, sexuality, intelligence. In our ungratefulness and falling short of full obedience, we are given an invitation to repent.

Rupert E. Davies has written:

> Fallen man still has the law of God written on his hearts, and a conscience with which to discern it. He knows what is right, but he is unable to do it. The first effect of such knowledge is to indicate to him the terrible doom which his sin incurs; but, since the purposes of God even in condemnation are loving, it goes on to show him his urgent need of Jesus Christ, and leads him toward Him. [Wesley taught his preachers] to preach the law first, and then the Gospel, the Law to open men's eyes to their dreadful predicament

and then to show them the way of escape, the Gospel to enable them to use it. Conscience . . . Wesley calls it 'prevenient grace,' . . . shows that God is at work even in depraved man for his salvation. So also is reason, and reason is not entirely withdrawn from fallen man. And he has another gift of God, perhaps the most precious gift of all, freedom. This freedom is not the natural right of fallen man. On the contrary, man forfeited his right to freedom, along with all his other rights, when he fell into sin. But God, of His mercy, has given us a measure of freedom, and by His grace we are able to perform our duty, and above all to hear and receive the Word of God (Davies 1976, 85).

Prevenient grace allows all persons to come to the realization (conviction) that they have sinned and fallen short and are in need of the saving and forgiving grace of God in Jesus Christ. Simply put, after all the rationalizations of what caused sin and who is the most or least sinful, Wesley's view of salvation is that the cause of sin is not traceable to the genes—that is, our inherited predilection to be greedy and self-serving—but the reason we sin and fall short of God's promise for us is that we choose to sin and will continue to until our hearts are changed from cold to warm.

Justifying Grace is God's undeserved, unjustified, unworthy gift of life through Christ Jesus, Ephesians 2:8-9:

For by grace you have been saved through faith, and this is not your own doing; it is the gift of God—not the result of works, so that no one may boast.

As outlined in John Wesley's sermon "The Lord our Righteousness":

These things must necessarily go together in our justification: upon God's part his great mercy and grace, upon Christ's part the satisfaction of God's justice, and on our part faith in the merits of Christ (Wesley 1991, 386).

Sanctifying and Perfecting Grace is the renewing gift of God's grace in Christ Jesus whereby our heart is changed and we love our neighbor without restrictions and with perfect intention.

This three-fold doctrine of grace—*prevenient, justifying, sanctifying and perfecting*—is further subdivided into *prevenient grace,* invitation, repentance; *justifying grace,* pardon and assurance; and *sanctifying and perfecting grace,* personal holiness and social holiness.

*A selection of Charles Wesley's hymns in The United Methodist Hymnal, 1989, illustrating Wesley's Theological and Lyrical elaborations of God's Grace in Jesus Christ.*

### Prevenient Grace—Invitation

"Come, sinners to the gospel feast" (**339**)

No one is excluded. Note the paraphrase in stanza 3 of Luke 14:16-24, the parable of the great dinner. "The invitation should be open to all, the crippled, the blind, and the lame, because they are not able to repay you."

### Prevenient Grace—Repentance

"Depth of mercy" (**355**)

Based on 1 Timothy 1:15, "The saying is sure and worthy of full acceptance, that Christ Jesus came into the world to save sinners—of whom I am the foremost." This theme is reiterated in stanza 1:7, "The chief of sinners." Stanza 3 reflects our daily crucifixion of Jesus, Hebrews 6:6b: "since on their own they are crucifying again the Son of God and are holding him up to contempt."

Stanza 5 is one of the most eloquent poetic paraphrases of Wesleyan evangelical piety; note particularly 5:3, "God is love! I *know*, I *feel*."

### Justifying Grace—Pardon

"And can it be that I should gain" (**363**)

This is one of two autobiographical hymns that Wesley composed at or near his conversion; the other is "Where shall my wondering soul begin" **(342)**. It is not known which of the two hymns Charles makes reference to in his *Journal* entry of May 23, 1738, "At nine I began a hymn on my conversion but was persuaded to break off for fear of pride. . . . I prayed Christ to stand by me and finished the hymn."

The poem is in 88.88.88, a meter often employed by Charles Wesley for the exposition of a major statement of faith. Frank Baker has commented on Wesley's metrical preference:

> The most prolific of all was his favourite form of six 8's— 8.8.8.8.8.8., rhyming ABABCC. In this metre he composed over 1,100 poems [a tenth of his entire output], a total of nearly 23,000 lines, most of them with a vigour, a flexibility, yet a disciplined compactness, that proved this to be the instrument fittest for his hand (Baker 1962, 45).

The hymn was published in six stanzas in *Hymns and Sacred Poems*, 1739, under the heading "Free Grace." It has been included in most Methodist hymnals, using either four or five stanzas; it is included in the 1989 hymnal in five stanzas. In stanza 1:6 "God has been changed from "Lord." The original stanza 5 has been omitted since John Wesley excluded it from his 1780 *Collection*:

> Still the small inward voice I hear,
>     That whispers all my sins forgiven;
> Still the atoning blood is near,
>     That quench'd the wrath of hostile heaven:
> I feel the life his wounds impart;
> I feel my Savior in my heart.

Five questions are posed at the hymn's opening, which establish a feeling of urgency that proceeds unrelentingly through this remarkable confession and "an extraordinary and daring tour-de-force, both poetically and theologically" (Watson and Trickett 1988, 152). Oliver A. Beckerlegge states that the whole kenosis doctrine (emptying of self, see Philippians 2:5-11 and hymns **166-167**) is condensed into a single line at 3:3 (Wesley 1983, 323).

Wesley's ability to exegete and integrate biblical imagery in a lyrical style with his account of a new life in Christ is seen in the following:

Stanza 1:1-2, Matthew 26:28: "For this is my blood of the covenant, which is poured out for many for the forgiveness of sins."

Stanza 1:3-6, Romans 5:6-8: "For while we were still weak, at the right time Christ died for the ungodly. Indeed, rarely will anyone die for a righteous person—though perhaps for a good person someone might actually dare to die. But God proves his love for us in that while we still were sinners Christ died for us."

Stanza 2:3-6, 1 Peter 1:12: "things into which angels long to look." Prophets and even angels have sought to understand what God was doing for the redemption of the faithful.

Stanza 3:1-4, Philippians 2:6-8: "who, though he was in the form of God, did not regard equality with God as something to be exploited, but emptied himself, taking the form of a slave being born in human likeness."

Stanza 3:4, Romans 5:12-14: "Therefore, just as sin came into the world through one man, and death came through sin, and so death spread to all because all have sinned—sin was indeed in the world before the law, but sin is not reckoned when there is no law. Yet death exercised dominion from Adam to Moses, even over those whose sins were not like the transgression of Adam, who is a type of the one who was to come."

Stanza 3:5-6, Psalm 85:7: "Show us your steadfast love, O Lord, and grant us your salvation."

Stanza 4, Acts 12:7: "Suddenly an angel of the Lord appeared and a light shone in the cell. He tapped Peter on the side and woke him, saying, 'Get up quickly.' And the chains fell off his wrists"; 12:9, 10b: "Peter went out [of his cell] and followed him [the angel, to] . . . the iron gate that led into the city, it opened for them of its own accord."

Stanza 5:1, Romans 8:1: "There is therefore now no condemnation for those who are in Christ Jesus."

Stanza 5:2, 1 Corinthians 3:21-22; "So let no one boast about human leaders. For all things are yours, whether Paul or Apollo or Cephas or the world or life or death or the present or the future—all belong to you, and you belong to Christ, and Christ belongs to God."

Stanza 5:3, 1 Corinthians 15:22: "For as all die in Adam, so all will be made alive in Christ."

Stanza 5:4, Philippians 3:8c-9: "That I may gain Christ and be found in him, not having a righteousness of my own that comes from the law, but one that comes through faith in Christ, the righteousness from God based on faith."

Stanza 5:5, Hebrews 10:19-20: "Therefore, my friends, since we have confidence to enter the sanctuary by the blood of Jesus, by the new and living way that he opened for us through the curtain (that is, through his flesh)." James 4:17: "Love has been perfected among us in this: that we may have boldness on the day of judgment."

Stanza 5:6, 2 Timothy 4:8: "From now on there is reserved for me the crown of righteousness, which the Lord, the righteous judge, will give me on that day, and not only to me but also to all who have longed for his appearing." James 1:12: "Blessed is anyone who endures temptation. Such a one has stood the test and will receive the crown of life that the Lord has promised to those who love him." Revelation 2:10c: "Be faithful until death, and I will give you the crown of life."

Although "And can it be that I should gain" has been in Methodist hymnals for over two hundred years, as far as twentieth-century USA Methodists are concerned, it was seldom sung until Thomas Campbell's SAGINA, composed in 1825, was introduced in the 1960's, and then with the complaint from some as to the tune's fitness for the words and its inherit musical worth. In this latter regard Erik Routley has stated that there is "little inspiration in melody or harmony, and what there is has to be beaten out very thin in order to accommodate a word-repetition, which, associated with a text so monumentally intense, come near profanity" (Routley 1981, 84).

Justifying Grace—Assurance

"How can we sinners know" **(372)** is a great Methodist manifesto that describes a Christian's experience of assurance through the inward witness of the Spirit. John Wesley defined this as an inward impression on the soul that "I am a child of God," that "Jesus Christ has loved me and given himself for me"; and that "all my sins are blotted out." This experience is confirmed by the believer's own awareness that in some measure he/she shows the marks of the Spirit (Watson and Trickett 1988, 414).

The title "The Marks of Faith" ("for I carry the marks of Jesus branded on my body," Galatians 6:17b) is applied to the fruits of the Spirit: love, joy, peace, long suffering, goodness, faith, meekness, temperance (Galatians 5:22-23).

Stanza 2, peace
Stanza 3, love
Stanza 4, goodness
Stanza 5, meekness
Stanza 6, faith

> By this we know that we abide in him and he in us, because he has given us of his Spirit. And we have seen and do testify that the Father has sent his Son as the Savior of the world. God abides in those who confess that Jesus is the Son of God, and they abide in God. So we have known and believe that love God has for us (1 John 4:13).

Sanctifying and Perfecting Grace—Rebirth/New Creature

"Love divine, all loves excelling" **(384)**

The hymn is based on 2 Corinthians 5:17, "So if anyone is in Christ, there is a new creation: everything old has passed away; see, everything has become new!" The crucified and risen Christ is the head of the new creation into which the believer as a new creature is incorporated (Metzger and Murphy 1991, 254)—stanza 4, "finish then thy new creation." Stanza 2 was omitted by John Wesley and has never been included by British Methodists. In the 1935 Methodist hymnal the gift of the "second blessing" in 2:4 ("let us find that second rest" was altered to "promised rest") reflected that day's controversy over matters of spiritual superiority implicit in the Holiness movement from the blessing of new birth in Christ to the Resurrection. More importantly, however, 2:5 has been a point of controversy since Wesley's time.

Frank Baker comments on the controversial line in stanza 2:5, "Take away our power of sinning":

> It was this line particularly which impelled John Wesley and others to omit the second verse from their hymnbooks, since it implies an extreme view of Christian perfection—a subject on which Charles Wesley himself was very scathing in some of his later poems. The Rev. John Fletcher of Madeley suggested its alteration to 'Take away the love of sinning,' pertinently asking: 'Can God take away from us our *power* of sinning without taking away our power of free obedience?' (Baker 1962, 95)

In stanza 3 of "Hark! the herald angels sing" **(240)**, Wesley uses the imagery of a child's birth, the Messiah's birth, to state as succinctly as anywhere in his hymns the doctrine of our rebirth in Christ: 3:7-8, "born to raise us from the earth, born to give us second birth" (Original: "born to raise the sons of earth").

### Sanctifying and Perfecting Grace—Personal Holiness

This is a troublesome attribute of Wesley's theology of holiness— variously subtitled entire sanctification, perfecting grace, perfect love, or Christian perfection. For the Wesleys salvation was neither exclusively personal nor social, but always both, as evidenced in early Methodists' opposition to the dehumanizing slave trade and the cruel treatment of prisoners, and their establishing schools for coal miners' children and medical care for the poor. In USA Methodism holiness has primarily been taught and practiced as *either* individualist *or* social, with the hymns of the social gospel reflecting the latter emphasis. With an appreciation of Wesley's emphasis on our holistic response to the gospel, Geoffrey Wainwright writes that "positively formulated, perfection meant for Wesley the pure love of God and Neighbour" (Wainwright 1980, 461). In the 1989 *United Methodist Hymnal* the hymns of "Personal Holiness," **396-424**, and "Social Holiness," **225-450**, are placed within the general classification of "Sanctifying and Perfecting Grace."

"O for a heart to praise my God" (**417**)

This hymn is based on Psalm 51:10 and first appeared in eight stanzas under the scripture heading "Psalm 51:10 Make me a clean Heart, O GOD" in *Hymns and Sacred Poems*, 1742. The five stanzas follow that are included in most hymnals; the full text is found on page xx:

1. O for a **heart** to praise my God,
   a **heart** from sin set free,
   a **heart** that always feels thy blood
   so freely shed for me.

2. A **heart** resigned, submissive, meek,
   my great Redeemer's throne,
   where only Christ is heard to speak,
   where Jesus reigns alone.

3. A humble, lowly, contrite **heart**,
   believing, true, and clean,
   which neither life nor death can part
   from Christ who dwells within.

4. A **heart** in every thought renewed
   and full of love divine,
   perfect and right and pure and good,
   a copy, Lord, of thine.

5. Thy nature, gracious Lord, impart;
   come quickly from above;
   write thy new name upon my **heart**,
   thy new, best name of Love.

In this hymn Charles Wesley reads the psalm text,

> Create in me a clean heart, O God.
> and put a new and right spirit within me (Psalm 51:10),

from a New Testament perspective and transforms its meaning:

> Now the heart is clean because it is set free from sin, and
> Christ is to reign in it and have his name written on it. . . .
> With its reference to the indwelling Christ . . . Ephesians
> 3:14-19 ["that Christ may dwell in your hearts through
> faith, as you are being rooted and grounded in love," verse
> 17] (one of Charles Wesley's most frequently-used pas-
> sages) is an important source for this hymn (Watson and
> Trickett 1988, 317).

The gift of the new heart is defined and elaborated in each stanza:

> Stanza 1, free from sin, a feeling heart
> Stanza 2, a submissive, serving heart
> Stanza 3, meek, contrite, humble heart
> Stanza 4, a renewed heart, full of love, perfect, pure, good, a copy
> of Christ's
> Stanza 5, a prayer for Christ to write a new name on the heart; the
> name is love.

### Sanctifying and Perfecting Grace—Social Holiness

Wesley texts explicitly stating the social imperatives of the gospel
were seldom published and consequently have not been included in our
hymnals. This exclusion has caused Charles Wesley's hymns of personal and individual response to the gospel to be perceived as his sole interest and preoccupation.

S T Kimbrough, Jr., comments on this development in the introduction to his collection of Wesley texts on social concerns, *A Song for the
Poor*.

The selection of his texts in most hymnals reflects strong doctrinal statements often embedded in an intense inner spiritual journey and in an evangelical-sacramental theology. The Wesley hymns that survive in hymnals also tend to reflect a "spiritualized" concept of "the poor." . . . [Therefore] the church's memory of Charles Wesley's message to the poor is minuscule at best . . . [since they omit] his texts that wed evangelization and socialization of the poor . . . the paradigm of faith that integrates head, heart, and hands (Kimbrough 1993, 14, 16).

It was not until the advent of the late-nineteenth and early-twentieth-century social gospel hymn that these concerns were brought into congregational song, but unfortunately in liberalism's critique of revivalism, they were presented as a remedy for the perceived antisocial, private, and personal responses to the gospel in all first-person pronoun hymns.

One of the few social holiness Wesley texts included in contemporary hymnals is stanza 4 of "Jesus, the gift divine I know" from *Short Hymns on Select Passages of the Holy Scriptures*, 1762, at 318 in *Hymns and Psalms*. It is based on James 1:27: "Pure religion and undefiled before God rather is this, To visit the fatherless and widow in their affliction and to keep himself unspotted from the world."

> Thy mind throughout my life be shown,
> > While listening to the sufferer's cry,
> The widow's and the orphan's groan,
> > On mercy's wings I swiftly fly,
> The poor and helpless to relieve,
> My life, my all, for them to give.

A second example from *A Song for the Poor* is "Your duty let the apostle show," based on the account of the first Christians sharing their possessions in Acts 4:34-35. The second stanza follows:

> Of your abundant store
>     you may few relieve.
> but all to feed the poor
>     you cannot, cannot give,
> houses and lands for Christ forego,
> or live as Jesus lived below.

Another hymn of social holiness which addresses the injustice of war is "Our earth we now lament to see" **(449)**. It was originally published under the title "For peace" in *Hymns of Intercession for All Mankind*, 1758. John Wesley placed it in the section on "Believers interceding for the world" in his 1780 *Collection*. The poem is one of the most moving expressions of the horror of war, and the soulful petition to God as Friend asks that the murder in our hearts be transformed to acts of kindness, and that the nations of the earth might join to form God's reign of righteousness, making for all "a paradise of perfect love!"

> 1.  Our earth we now lament to see
>         with floods of wickedness overflowed,
>     with violence, wrong, and cruelty,
>         one wide-extended field of blood,
>     where men like fiends each other tear
>     in all the hellish rage of war.
>
> 2.  As listed on Abaddon's side,
>         they mangle their own flesh, and slay;
>     Tophet is moved, and opens wide
>         its mouth for it enormous prey;
>     and myriads sink beneath the grave,
>     and plunge into the flaming wave.
>
> 3.  O might the universal Friend
>         the havoc of his creatures see!
>     Bid our unnatural discord end,
>         declare us reconciled in thee!
>     Write kindness on our inward parts
>     and chase the murderer from our hearts!

4. Who now against each other rise,
      the nations of the earth constrain
   to follow after peace, and prize
      the blessings of thy righteous reign,
   the joys of unity to prove,
   the paradise of perfect love!

The second stanza includes Satanic images from the depths of Sheol, drawn from Revelation 9:11:

They have as king over them the angel of the bottomless pit; his name in Hebrew is Abaddon [Destruction], and in Greek he is called Apollyon [Destroyer].

Victor R. Gold and William L Holladay comment that the images also express the violent death and destruction of the defilers of God in Jeremiah 7:30-34:

The most gruesome of Israel's aberrations was the sacrifice of children (19:5; 32:35) on the burning platform (Topheth, 2 Kings 23:10). Strictly forbidden by God (Lev. 18:21), it will eventually be recognized as murder (Metzger and Murphy 1991, 974).

The poet's vast repertory of scriptural metaphor and detail is demonstrated in his reference to Topheth, the sacred place that Jeremiah states will become the burying ground, i.e., the "valley of Slaughter."

### Charles Wesley, Commentator and Music Critic

Charles's views on church music were basically formed through his knowledge of and fidelity to the worship and liturgical music of the Anglican church and church schools, and they often complemented his brother's pragmatic ideals. In stanza five of a poem in *Hymns and Sacred Poems*, 1749, he joins his brother's warning against music's power to distract the faithful:

Still let us on our guard be found,
And watch against the power of sound
   With sacred jealousy;
Lest haply sense should damp our zeal.
And music's charms bewitch and steal
   Our hearts away from thee.

Along with his leanings towards traditional church music, Charles apparently also had a flexible approach to appropriate musical settings of his poems. For example, a pub tune (folk melody) was central to Charles Wesley's writing "The True Use of Musik." According to Frank Baker (1962, 117), the text was probably composed to the tune "Nancy Dawson," similar to "Here we go 'round the mulberry bush," and sung in response to a company of half-drunken sailors who had interrupted Charles's open-air preaching service in Plymouth, 1746. It was first included in *Hymns and Sacred Poems*, 1749, and appeared with the tune EPWORTH in Thomas Butts's *Harmonia Sacra*, ca. 1756; a later version appeared in 1769 and in 1805 in the USA in Jeremiah Ingalls' *Christian Harmony* under the title "Innocent Sounds."

The 1749 version is included from Baker 1962, 118.

1.  Listed into the Cause of Sin,
     Why should a Good be Evil?
  Musick, alas! too long has been
     Prest to obey the Devil:
  Drunken, or lewd, or light the Lay
     Flow'd to the Soul's Undoing,
  Widen'd, and strew'd with Flowers the Way
     Down to Eternal Ruin.

2.  Who on the Part of God will rise,
     *Innocent Sound* recover,
  Fly on the Pray, and take the Prize,
     Plunder the Carnal Lover,
  Strip him of every moving Stain,
     Every melting Measure,
  Musick in Virtue's Cause retain,
     Rescue the Holy Pleasure?

3.  Come let us try if JESU'S Love
     Will not as well inspire us:
    This is the Theme of Those above,
     This upon Earth shall fire us.
    Say, if your Hearts are tun'd to sing,
     Is there a Subject greater?
    Harmony all its Strains may bring,
     JESUS'S Name is sweeter.

4.  JESUS the Soul of Musick is;
     His is the Noblest Passion:
    JESUS'S Name is Joy and Peace,
     Happiness and Salvation:
    JESUS'S Name the dead can raise,
     Shew us our Sins forgiven,
    Fill us with all the Life of Grace,
     Carry us up to Heaven.

The education and promotion of the careers of his sons fostered another facet of Charles's musical orientation and brought increased contact with royalty, nobility, patrons, and the musical establishment, particularly after his move to London in 1771. This interaction had apparently begun in the mid-1740's (see page 108) when Mrs. Rich presumably introduced Charles to Lampe. Lampe in turn may have introduced the Wesleys to G. F. Handel; and according to Charles (Wesley 1849, 2:142) introduced Charles, Jr., to Handel's music. Mrs. Rich also encouraged the musical training of Charles, Jr., by "giving him Handel's songs" (Wesley 1849, 2:142).

About the time of Wesley's move from Bristol to London, Jonathan Battishill, 1738-1801, a theater composer and conductor, leading church organist, and composer of anthems, glees and songs, set twelve of Charles's hymns from *Hymns and Sacred Poems*, 1749.

> *Twelve Hymns*, The Words by the Revd. Mr. Charles Wesley M.A. Late Student of Christ Church, Oxford. Set to Music by Mr. Jonathan Battishill. London. Printed for the Author by C and S Thompson in St. Paul's Church Yard. Where may be had by the same Author The Favourite Songs in the Opera of Almena. Price 3S.

Battishill's settings are highly ornamented melodies, presumably for a trained singer, with figured bass accompaniment. The collection is number 138.vi, dated ca. 1779, in Frank Baker's Union Catalogue. There are two extant copies, one in the Methodist Archives Library, Drew University, Madison, New Jersey, and the other in the library of the Divinity School, Duke University, Raleigh, North Carolina. S T Kimbrough, Jr. has provided the present writer a photocopy of the former. See also "John Wesley and Popular Music," page 104, for a discussion of John F. Lampe's settings of Charles's hymns for solo voice.

From 1779 to 1786, in his London Chesterfield Street home, he presented annual subscription concerts to promote his sons' careers. Sunday performances featured only sacred music.

> A large room was set apart and suitably equipped. The ticket for a series was three guineas and regular subscribers numbered from thirty to fifty. . . . [Expense] items for a concert in 1786 amounted to £1.11.6 and included: apples 4/6, organ 3—, wine 4/2, tea 3/, sugar 3/, cream, 1/—, lemons 1/—. On these occasions, which were well patronized and yielded a small profit, young Charles played on the organ and his brother the violoncello. Among those present were the Lord mayor and the Bishop of London, and on one occasion Uncle John himself, somewhat reluctantly and, as he confessed, a little out of his element, though he spent an agreeable hour, but preferred plain music and plain company (Gill 1964, 190).

Word of the concerts brought harsh criticism from evangelicals including the Anglican poet William Cowper and Methodist leaders John Fletcher and Thomas Coke. Charles in a letter to John defended the concerts as "the will and order of Providence." John, who had great affection for his nephews, printed the letter in *The Armenian Magazine*, "with the dry comment that the concerts were hardly in the order of Providence, that he was of another mind and thought they increased spiritual dangers" (Gill 1964, 191), to which Charles listed in a letter to John "My reasons for letting my sons have a concert:"

1. To keep them out of harm's way; the way, (I mean) of bad music and bad musicians, who by a free communication with them might corrupt both their taste and their morals.

2. That my sons may have a safe and honourable opportunity of availing themselves of their musical abilities, which have cost me several hundred pounds.

3. That they may enjoy their full right of private judgment, and likewise their independency, both of which must be given up if they swim with the stream and follow the multitude.

4. To improve their play and their skill in composing; as they must themselves furnish the principal music of every concert.

The *Wesley/Langshaw Correspondence*, edited by Arthur W. Wainwright in collaboration with Don E. Saliers, provides new evidence of Charles's musical activity and interests, including his characterization of London musicians in a 1779 letter to John Langshaw with this advice for Langshaw's musician-son:

Send Jack a word of Advice (which we may second) constantly to attend the Church Service on Sunday—which almost the whole tribe of Musicians neglect (Wainwright 1993, 32-33).

Charles's move to London afforded him a more sustained contact with music making and musicians of his day, which served to increase the concert activity and visibility of his two sons. For example, his younger son Samuel became the protégé of Martin Madan (see page 111), and Charles, Jr. began to attract private students. Some of this interaction was expressed by Charles in poems composed for the moment. They afford valuable insight into his subtle and at times ascerbic humor, and his impressive grasp of issues related to musical style and performance-practice. In this latter regard some poems reflect the resistance to the introduction of instruments from the continent by music patrons and performers in London's concert halls and theaters. Charles's conservative musical tastes were shared by Joseph Kelway, organist at St. Martin-in-the-Fields, London, who taught Charles, Jr., for two years without accepting any payment, and whom the poet obviously held in high esteem.

The first is about the encroachment of continental modern music from MS Patriotism: Misc., pp. 6-7, that Frank Baker included at 312 in *Representative Verse of Charles Wesley*, now out of print. This poem and several others included in this text may be found in *The Unpublished Poetry of Charles Wesley*.

## MODERN MUSIC

G [iardini], B [Johann Christian Bach], and all
their followers, great and small,
Have cut Old Music's throat,
And mangled every Note;
Their superficial pains
have dash'd out all his brains:
And now we doat upon
A lifeless sceleton,
The empty sound at most,
The Squeak of Music's Ghost.

His satirical criticism of the pianoforte included in Baker (1962, 362-63) from MS Patriotism: Misc., pp. 13-15, demonstrates a thorough understanding of the forces in mid-eighteenth-century British music, its performance style, personages, and taste.

## THE PIANOFORTE
## WRITTEN IN THE YEAR 1783

Our Connoisseurs their plausive voices raise,
And dwell on the PIANO-FORTE'S praise.
More brilliant (if we simply take their word)
More sweet than any tinkling Harpsichord,

While soothing Softness and Expression meet
To make the Contrast, and the joy compleat.
To strike our fascinated ears and eyes
And take our Sense and Reason by surprise.

'Tis thus the men whose dictates we obey,
Their taste, and their Authority display,
Command us humbly in their steps to move,
Damn what they damn, & praise what they approve,
With Faith implicit, and with blind esteem,
To own—All Music is ingross'd by Them.

So the gay Nation whose capricious law
Keeps the whole fashionable world in awe,
Nor to Italian Airs their ear incline,
Nor to the noblest Harmony divine,
But as the Sum of Excellence propose
Their own sweet Sonnets—warbled thro' the Nose!

Yet skilful Masters of the tuneful string,
(Masters who teach the Harpsichord to—*sing*)
Tell us of Music's powers a different story,
And rob PIANO-FORTE of its glory;
Assuring us, if uncontroul'd by Fashion,
We hear, and judge without exaggeration,
The Merit of the favourite instrument,
And all its Use and musical intent,
By the discerning Few is understood
'To hide bad Players, & spoil the Good.'

　　Second Part

What cannot Fashion do? with magic ease
It makes the dull Piano-forte please,
Bids us a triffling Instrument admire,
As far superior to Apollo's Lyre:
Loud as a spanking Warming-pan its tone,
Delicious as the thrilling Bagpipe's Drone.

Organs and Harpsichords it sweeps away
And reigns alone, triumphant for a day:
The Great acknowledge its inchanting power
The echoing multitude of course adore:
Ev'n Those who *real* Music dared esteem
Caught for a while, are carried down the stream,
O'er all her slaves while Fashion domineers,
A Midas lends them his sagacious Ears!

Shou'd Fashion singling out (if that could be)
A poorer tool of modern harmony
The sanction of her approbation give;
The world polite her dictates wou'd receive,
The list'ning Herd wou'd fall with awe profound
And die transported at a JEWS-HARP'S Sound!

In this stunning satire from MS Patriotism: Misc., pp. 6-7 (included by Beckerlegge and Kimbrough 1990, 3:382), traditional musical style combining sound and sense, which Kelway personified, is compared with modern music and its predilection to confuse.

WRITTEN IN KELWAY'S SONATAS

Kelway's Sonatas who can bear?
'They want both harmony and air;
Heavy they make the Player's hand
And who their tricks can understand?
Kelway to the profound G [Giardini, or J. C. Bach]
Or B[Boyce] compared, is but a Ninny,
A Dotard old (the Moderns tell ye)
Mad after Handel and Corelli,
Spoilt by original disaster,
For Geminiani was his Master,
And taught him, in his nature's ground
To gape for Sense, as well as sound.'
'Tis thus the Leaders of our nation,
Smit with the Music now in fashion,

Their absolute decisions deal,
And from the chair Infallible,
And praise the fine, Italian Taste,
Too fine, too exquisite to last.

Let Midas judge, and what will follow?
A whis[t]ling Pan excels Apollo,
A Bag-pipe's sweeter than an Organ,
A Sowgelder* surpasses Worgan**
And Kelway at the foot appears
Of Connoisseurs—with Asses ears!

\*    A maker and master of Castratos
\*\*  John Worgan, organist and composer, tutor to Charles, Jr.

His similar views are expressed in this cleverly constructed 88.88. 88. 99. 88 verse.

### ANOTHER

Who'er admires as Excellence
Sound unaccompanied by Sense,
Shall have my free consent to praise
The favourite Music of our days.
Still let them dance to Orpheus' Sons
Who captivate the Stocks and Stones;
And while (to harmony's confusion)
The Masters show their execution
Attend with long transported ears,
Bad Music's Executioners.

Charles frequently attended the theater, the opera, and other musical events (see 104, 107 for a discussion of the Wesleys' association with theater patrons). In the following poem he extols the successful concert tour of Cecilia Davies, known in Italy as L'Inglesina, a popular eighteenth-century vocalist and the first Englishwoman to appear on the Italian stage. Wesley probably wrote these lines found in the MS, loose sheet, Lamplough Collection, during her first British tour, when she was still thoroughly Italianized (Baker 1962, 327).

TO MISS DAVIS

Gentle Inglesina, say
Can the smooth Italian Lay
Nature's ruggedness remove,
Soften Britons into love?
Yes; the stocks & stones draw near,
Thy inchanting Voice to hear
And all the Savages agree
In praise of harmony & Thee!

In this social context Charles also met John F. Lampe, a German associate of G. F. Handel and a prominent operatic composer. Because of Charles's relationship with Lampe (see pages 107-08), it is quite possible (Martin 1985, 73) that his poem "The Musician's Hymn," number 25 in *Hymns for those that seek and those that have Redemption in the Blood of Jesus Christ* (London, 1747), was composed to celebrate the composer's conversion by John Wesley, who entered in his *Journal* for Friday, November 29, 1745, "I spent an hour with Mr. Lampe, who had been a Deist for many years, till it pleased God, by the *Earnest Appeal* [*to Men of Reason and Religion*, 1743] to bring him to a better mind" (Wesley 1938, 3:226).

1.  Thou God of harmony and love,
    Whose name transports the saints above,
        And lulls the ravish'd spheres:
    On Thee in feeble strains I call,
    And mix my humble voice with all
        The heavenly chorister.

2.  If well I know the tuneful art
    To captivate a human heart,
        The glory, Lord, be Thine:
    A servant of Thy blessed will,
    I here devote my utmost skill
        To sound the praise Divine.

3.  With *Tubal's* wretched Sons no more
    I prostitute my sacred Powers,
        To please the Fiends beneath;
    Or modulate the wanton Lay,
    Or smooth with Musick's Hand the way
        To everlasting death.

4.  Suffice for this the season past:
    I come, great God, to learn at last
        The lesson of thy grace;
    Teach me the new, the gospel song,
    And let my hand, my heart, my tongue
        Move only to thy praise.

5.  Thine own musician, Lord, inspire,
    And let my consecrated lyre
        Repeat the psalmist's part:
    His Son and thine reveal in me,
    And fill with sacred melody
        The fibers of my heart.

6.  So shall I charm the listening throng,
    And draw the living stones along,
        by Jesus' tuneful name:
    The living stones shall dance, shall rise,
    And form a city in the skies,
        The *New Jerusalem!*

7.  O might I with Thy saints aspire,
    The meanest of that dazzling choir,
        Who chant Thy praise above;
    Mix'd with the bright musician-band,
    May I an heavenly harper stand,
        And sing the song of love.

8.  What ecstasy of bliss is there,
    While all the' angelic concert share,
        And drink the floating joys!
    What more than ecstasy, when all
    Struck to the golden pavement fall
        At Jesu's glorious voice!

9. Jesus, the heaven of heaven He is,
The soul of harmony and bliss!
    And while on Him we gaze,
And while His glorious voice we hear,
Our spirits are all eye, all ear,
    And silence speaks His praise.

10. O might I die that awe to prove,
That prostrate awe which dares not move,
    Before the great Three-One;
To shout by turns the bursting joy,
And all eternity employ
    In songs around the throne.

To commemorate Lampe's death Charles composed this poem in the same 88. 88. 88 meter:

### ON THE DEATH OF MR. LAMPE

1. 'Tis done! the Sovereign will's obey'd,
The soul, by angel-guards convey'd,
    Has took its seat on high;
The brother of my choice is gone
To music sweeter than his own,
    And concerts in the sky.

2. His spirit, mounting on the wing,
Rejoiced to hear the convoy sing,
    While harping at his side:
With ease he caught their heavenly strain,
And smiled and sung in mortal pain,
    He sung, and smiled, and died.

3. Enroll'd with that harmonious throng,
He hears the'unutterable song,
    The'unutterable name:
He *sees* the Master of the choir,
He bows, and strikes the golden lyre,
    And hymns the glorious Lamb.

4.  He hymns the glorious Lamb *alone*;
    No more constrain'd to make his moan
        In this sad wilderness,
    To toil for sublunary pay,
    And cast his sacred strains away,
        And stoop the world to please.

5.  Redeem'd from earth, the tuneful soul,
    While everlasting ages roll,
        His triumph shall prolong;
    His noblest faculties exert,
    And all the music of his heart
        Shall warble on his tongue.

6.  O that my mournful days were past!
    O that I might o'ertake at last
        My happy friend above;
    With him the church triumphant join,
    And celebrate in strains divine
        The majesty of love!

7.  Great God of love, prepare my heart,
    And tune it now to bear a part
        In heavenly melody:
    "I'll strive to sing as loud as they,
    Who sit enthroned in brighter day,"
        And nearer the Most high.

8.  O that the promised time were come!
    O that we all were taken home
        Our Master's joy to share!
    Draw, Lord, the living vocal stones,
    Jesus, recall Thy banish'd ones,
        To chant Thy praises there.

9.  Our number and our bliss complete,
    And summon all the choir to meet
        Thy glorious throne around;
    Thy whole musician-band bring in,
    And give the signal to begin,
        And let the trumpet sound.

(Wesley 1849, 2:408-09; undated. Lampe died July 25, 1751.)

Charles, more than his brother John, apparently moved with ease and more frequently among London's theater musicians and patrons and came in contact with many famous personages, including George F. Handel (see page 171, "John F. Lampe" and Charles Wesley's account in his *Journal* (Wesley 1849, 140-66) of the musical training of his two sons, and *Wesley/Langshaw Correspondence).* Between 1749 and 1752, Handel composed three settings for Charles Wesley's hymns for solo voice and figured bass: ON THE RESURRECTION for "Rejoice! the Lord is King" (Tune: GOPSAL, *The United Methodist Hymnal,* **716**); THE INVI-TATION for "Sinners, obey the gospel word"; and DESIRING TO LOVE for "O Love divine, how sweet thou art." The original manuscripts were discovered in 1826 in the Fitzwilliam Museum Library at Cambridge by the poet's son Samuel, who in turn published them as *The Fitzwilliam Music never before Published, Three Hymns, the Words by the late Rev. Charles Wesley . . . Set to Music by George Frideric Handel . . . 1826.* A monograph was published by Novello in 1988.

Frank Baker includes two tributes to Handel, at page 311, in *The Representative Verse of Charles Wesley*: The first is from MS Patriotism: Misc., p. 5, and second from MS E. T. Clark.

### ODE ON HANDEL'S BIRTHDAY
### S. MATTHIAS DAY FEBR[UARY] 24

Hail the bright auspicious Day
   That gave Immortal Handel birth.
Let every moment glide away
   In solemn joy and sacred mirth;
Let every soul like his aspire
And catch a glowing spark of pure etherial fire.

### WRITTEN IN HANDEL'S LESSONS

Here all the mystic Powers of sound,
The soul of Harmony is found,
Its perfect Character receives,
And Handel dead for ever lives!

The following poem from MS Patriotism: Misc., p. 11 (Baker 1962, 312), was apparently composed to defend his fostering his son's musical ambitions, activity that some Methodists, including John Fletcher, opposed. In 1775 Fletcher wrote Wesley: "You have your enemies, as well as your brother. They complain of your love for music, the company of fine people, great folks, and of the want of your former zeal and frugality. I need not put you in mind to cut off all sinful appearances" (Gill 1964, 190).

> Men of true piety, they know not why,
> Music with all its sacred powers decry,
> Music itself (not its abuse) condemn,
> For good or bad is just the same to Them.
> But let them know, They quite mistake the Case,
> Defect of nature for excess of grace:
> and, while they reprobate th'harmonious Art,
> Blam'd we excuse, and candidly assert
> The fault is in their ear, not in their upright heart.

Charles's appreciation for his talented sons' musical advances as compared with his own lack of formal training is the theme of this poem that Frank Baker transcribed from the poet's shorthand and included at page 311 in *The Representative Verse of Charles Wesley*:

> Who would not wish to have the skill
>  Of tuning instruments at will?
> Ye powers who guide my actions, tell
> Why I, in whom the seeds of music dwell,
> Who most its power and excellence admire,
> Whose very breast itself a lyre
> Was never taught the happy art
>  Of modulating sounds
> And can no more in concert share a part
> Than the wild roe that o'er the mountains bounds.

The poet described the beginning of Samuel's musical training for Daines Barrington who first heard him play in 1775, when the boy was nine years of age (Baker 1962, 330).

ON SAMUEL WESLEY

Sam for his three first years the Secret kept,
While in his heart the Seed of Music slept,
Till Charles's Chissel by a carnal Stroke
Brought for the Statue latent in the block:
Like Memmon then, he caught the Solar Fire,
And breath'd spontaneous to Apollo's lyre,
With nature's ease th'Harmonious Summit won
The envious, and the gazing Croud outrun,
Left all the rest behind, & seizd on—Barrington.

In the early 1770's Charles petitioned William Boyce, the celebrated eighteenth-century English church musician, composer, and compiler of the monumental and influential three-volume *Cathedral Music* (1760, 1768, 1773), to take his son Samuel into his choir and to present him with the three-volume work as a gift. Evidently Charles had deep respect for Boyce, whom he states set some of his hymns. Nicholas Temperley has discovered:

> [A] Boyce setting in G Major of 'Servant of God, well done' that was published with a four-voice tune by Charles Wesley, Jr., about 1795, with the heading: "Written by the Revd. Charles Wesley on the Death of the Revd. George Whitefield. Set to music by the late Dr. Boyce, Composer to His Majesty" (Correspondence with Carlton R. Young, April 1994).

Boyce, who had praised Samuel's early compositions by calling him "an English Mozart" (Wesley 1849, 2:154), also represented Charles's penchant for the cathedral-music tradition he experienced during his student days at Westminster School, adjacent to the Abbey where William Croft served as organist. Charles later stated that his son Charles received from his uncle, presumably John Wesley, the "inestimable present of Dr. Boyce's Cathedral Music" (Wesley 1849, 2:144).

The poem to Boyce is included at vol. 1:279 in Oliver A. Beckerlegge's and S T Kimbrough, Jr.'s *Unpublished Poetry of Charles Wesley*:

1.  The humble Petition
    Of a rhiming Musician,
        (A Petition of Natural Right)
     Undeniably shews
    That, wherever he goes,
        Church-Music is all his delight:

2.  That he never can rest,
    Till enrich'd with the best,
        His Talent aright he employs,
    And claims for his own,
     A True Harmony's Son,
        The Collection of good Doctor Boyce.

3.  Three Volumes of yours,
    Which his Prayer procures,
        Will afford him Examples enough,
    And save Poet Sam
    (Your petitioner's Name)
        From a Deluge of Musical Stuff.

4.  So, good Doctor, if now
    His suit you allow,
        And make him as rich as a king,
    Taken into your Choir,
    To his Organ and Lyre,
        Your Petitioner ever shall—Sing!

Following the composer's death, February 7, 1779, Charles composed this lyrical remembrance that is included at 2:410 in his *Journal*.

1.   Father of harmony, farewell!
       Farewell for a few fleeting years!
     Translated from the mournful vale
       Jehovah's flaming ministers
     Have borne thee to thy place above,
     Where all is harmony and love.

2.   Thy generous, good and upright heart,
       Which sigh'd for a celestial lyre,
     Was tuned on earth to bear a part
       Symphonious with the heavenly choir,
     Where Handel strikes the warbling strings,
     And plausive angels clap their wings.

3.   Handel, and all the tuneful train,
       Who well employ'd their art divine
     To' announce the great Messiah's reign,
       In joyous acclamations join,
     And, springing from their azure seat,
     With shouts their new-born brother greet.

4.   Thy brow a radiant circle wears,
       Thy hand a golden harp receives,
     And, singing with the morning stars,
       Thy soul in endless raptures lives,
     And hymns, on the eternal throne,
     Jehovah and His conquering Son.

Charles also encouraged the musical training of his wife, Sally, who "used to quiet and amuse him [Charles, Jr.] with the harpsichord" (see pages 108-09). Frederick Gill comments that Sally "played the harpsichord and had a fine, though not strong singing voice . . . [and at age eighty] sang to her friend's astonishment two of Handel's songs most delightfully—'He shall feed his flock,' etc. and 'If God be with us,' etc." (Gill 1964, 192). Her son Charles states that at age ninety-six his mother "Sang an Air, on her Birth day last week" (Wainwright 1993, 74).

Two additional poems, "On the Death of Charles Worgan," who was the son of the famous organist, John Worgan, and "An Epistle to Dr. Ludlow" (Baker 1962, 324-25), the latter perhaps by his son Samuel, further demonstrate Charles Wesley's natural and acquired musical sensitivities as expressed in this sampling of his poems about music and musicians.

## ON THE DEATH OF CHARLES WORGAN, AGED 17 OR 18

1.  Blooming Innocent, adieu!
        Lovely, transitory Flower,
    Faded is the youthful hue,
        Ended is thy morning hour!
    Death hath seal'd thy sleeping eyes—
    Open'd now in paradise!

2.  Ravish'd hence by Sovereign Love,
        Wing'd with empyrean fire,
    Soars thy soul to realms above,
        Mingles with the immortal quire
    Hears the Music of the Spheres,
    All the heavenly Harpers hears.

3.  Happy harmonist, to Thee
        Sovereign Love assigns a Place,
    Crowns thy spotless purity,
        Decks thy head with brighter rays,
    Bids thee join the Virgin throng,
    Chant th'inimitable Song.

4.  Passing thro' this mortal Vale,
        Lo, we after Thee aspire,
    Where Thou dost their triumphs swell,
        Raise their highest raptures higher;
    Sing the glorious One in Three,
    Shout thro' all eternity.

The following poem addressed to the Bristol surgeon, Abraham Ludlow, was apparently composed as a commentary on the comic-like situation that developed when Samuel Wesley, who was to substitute for his brother Charles in a benefit performance in the Bristol Cathedral on Thursday evening March 31, 1774, was set aside by the last-minute appearance of his older brother who apparently played the announced organ concerto—one of the evening's ninety-seven performers (Baker 1962, 325).

### AN EPISTLE TO DR. LUDLOW

1. To you, dear Doctor, I appeal,
      To all the Tuneful City.
   Am I not used extremely ill
      By Musical Committee?

2. Why 'tis enough to make one wild—
      They court, and then refuse me,
   They Advertize and call me Child,
      And as a Child they use me.

3. Excusing their contempt, they say
      (Which more inflames my passion)
   I am not grave enough to play
      Before the Corporation.

4. To the sweet City-waits altho'
      I may not hold a candle,
   I question if their Worships know
      The Odds t'wixt me and Handel.

5. A Child of 8 years old I grant,
   Must be both light & giddy,
   The Solidness of Burgum* want
   The Steadiness of Liddy*:

6. Yet quick perhaps as other folks
      I can assign a reason,
   And keep my time as well as Stokes*
      And come as much in season.

7.  With Bristol-Organists not yet
    I come in competition:
    But let them know I wou'd be great
    I do not want ambition.

8.  Spirit I do not want, or will
    Upon a just occasion,
    To Make the rash Despisers feel
    My weight of indignation.

9.  Tread on a worm, twill turn again:
    And shall not I resent it?
    Who gave the sore affront, in vain
    They wou'd with tears repent it.

10. Nothing shall, sir, appease my Rage
    At their uncouth demeanor,
    Unless they prudently assuage
    Mine anger with—A Steyner.**


*Burgum, Liddy (Lediard), and Stokes were friends of
Charles Wesley and patrons of the arts in Bristol.
** A Stainer violin made in Tyrol.

# 6. Afterword

This study began with an overview of evangelical Protestantism's religion of the heart and lyrical religion, and concluded with eighteenth-century Methodist music, music-making, and musicians in the activity of its principal leaders John and Charles Wesley—music of the heart. The Wesleys expressed their innate musicality in hymns, tune books, and commentary on music and joined the music of the heart with the religion of the heart into a lyrical theology that could be sung in contrasting musical performance practices often aided by choir and/or soloists in various settings, e.g., parish, chapel, and classes. Methodist lay preaching and lay-led music of the heart in revival settings in time became the primary means of publicly celebrating God's redeeming grace in Jesus Christ—grace offered, experienced, and accepted. The joyous celebration of God's unexpected and unearned saving grace, concurrently personal and social, supplanted the monotony and apathy of morning and evening prayer and the privatism of the Eucharist. Here, Methodist hymn books became de facto prayer books and catechisms.

My expectation is that this volume will prompt additional research and commentary. One area for further study is the relationship in early Methodism of feeling, memory and music-making. The relationship of feeling with the musical response was expressed two centuries after the Wesleys by Carl E. Seashore in his monumental study *Psychology of Music*:

> Music is essentially a play upon feeling with feeling. It is appreciated only insofar as it arouses feeling and can be expressed only by active feeling. . . . To feel is always to do, to express something—[an] action of the organism. . . . The medium through which [the musician works] is feeling, not factual material objects or abstract philosophies (Seashore 1938, 9-10).

Wesley intuitively and pragmatically linked feeling, musical response and doctrinal teaching—the music of the heart. Music, with notable exceptions, e.g., John F. Lampe, was made by amateurs for amateurs. We have seen in the work and opinions of John Wesley, manager-pastor-guide of the movement, Methodism's dependence on lyrical religion to shape and maintain its mission and witness. Wesley appears to be convinced that because he could sing and lead singing and since God has given to all the gift of musicality, with instruction and encouragement all can and ought to be taught to sing their joyful and active response to God's saving grace in Jesus Christ. Wesley's brand of hymn singing, Erik Routley says, introduced "a problem and a tension which never disappears from hymnody . . . the problem of the counterpoint of reassurance and judgment, of freedom and authority (Routley 1981, 75).

Charles, who after his move in 1771 from Bristol to London maintained his relationships with Methodists at the Foundery and at City Road Chapel (Gill 1964, 183), had reservations "about the direction that the movement was taking" (Wainwright 1993, 6). At the same time, having found the necessary financial resources, he fostered his sons' training as professional musicians. In time they would become a part of that small group of composers, conductors, performers, and critics who because of their disciplined musical imagination and their elusive quest for musical perfection are usually removed from amateur music and music-making—the essence of Wesleyan-style congregational song.

Further research may reveal more about John's and Charles's later opinions about amateur and professional music and music-making, including Charles's relationship to the music and liturgy of London's Anglican churches, including Old Marylebone parish, and the Methodist chapels.

In another regard, I suspect that there is considerable more interaction of Methodist and Anglican performance practice and repertory than I have been able to uncover. I am intrigued with Robin Leaver's comment that evangelicals within the church, particularly the leaders of independent or proprietary chapels such as George Whitefield, Martin Madan, and Augustus Toplady, compiled hymnals that included Wesley hymns.

> What has generally gone unnoticed is the fact that the hymn collections of these other Anglican evangeli-

cals—largely, though not exclusively, Calvinistic in their theology—constitute a sequence of hymnal publication that parallels the "Methodist" collections of John and Charles Wesley (Kimbrough 1992, 168-69).

On the musical side, we have considered the theater-style tunes that John F. Lampe and Jonathan Battishill composed (see pages 106, 177,) and the anonymous tunes supplement appended to *Hymns and Sacred Poems*, Dublin, 1749 (see page 67). Were other Methodist-sponsored collections issued and used during Wesley's time? Did Methodists in Wesley's time encourage social singing? What was the relationship of Methodist singing practice to the village choir movement and singing schools?

While the developments in British Methodism following Wesley's death are beyond the scope of this study, I have briefly noted the dramatic changes in musical style and the increased use of organs and choirs. The minutes of Methodist conferences and the contents of the two tune collections of Charles Jr. and Samuel (see pages 80-82) seem likely places for further study of these developments. Charles Jr.'s collection was an apology for and a revision of his uncle's *Sacred Harmony*. Samuel, in *Original Hymn Tunes,* composed a tune for each of the meters of the hymns in his uncle's 1780 *Collection*. Samuel's work appears to be the first to provide Methodists, under the rubrics of modesty, musical refinement and good taste, with an alternative for the variety of styles represented in Wesley's tune books. His is an early example of efforts by nineteenth-century Anglican composers to combine proper and popular genteel musical style and good taste in tunes for parish congregations and choirs with organ accompaniment that became "not simply aids to congregational worship, [but] aspired to be works of art in their own right" (Temperley 1979, 304).

This approach to writing congregational music culminated in the hymn tunes of the professional church musicians, including Samuel's son Samuel Sebastian, who composed the musical settings for *Hymns Ancient and Modern*, 1861. This collection greatly influenced the British

Methodist Wesley's *Hymns and New Supplement*, 1877, a tunes edition that bears scant reference to the repertory in John Wesley's tune books.

A generation later Ralph Vaughan Williams' remarkable preface to the music of *The English Hymnal*, 1906, whose musical standards complemented the collection's literary upgrading, elevated the cause of taste in hymn tunes to a moral imperative, "It is indeed a moral rather than a musical issue" (Vaughan Williams 1906, ix).

A study comparing the work of John Wesley and Ralph Vaughan Williams might prove interesting since they both greatly expanded the tune repertory. Vaughan Williams introduced unison tunes (Wesley's essential point in "Thoughts on the Power of Music"); folk melody with their winsome and oft-times dance qualities; gospel hymns referenced, "Not For Ordinary Use"; and over strong objections of purists items such as the heart-felt Welsh melody AR HYD Y NOS. His unison Baroque trio-like SINE NOMINE offended Victorian musical sensitivities so that Bernard Lord Manning, who had dismissed Vaughan Williams' tunes as "jazz music," in the mid-1930's said, "Until it was set to a feeble dance tune [SINE NOMINE] by Vaughan Williams, Bishop How's 'For all the saints' was a hymn with merit" (Manning 1942, 36).

### *Authority in Church Music*

John Wesley as Methodism's prominent, articulate leader assumed his authority and pragmatically, scarcely systematically, shaped and articulated it from his aesthetic, pastoral, theological, and cultic concerns and opinions; see his introduction to *Sacred Melody* and his "Gamut," pages 74-75, "Directions for Singing," pages 72-73, "Thoughts on The Power of Music," pages 84-88, and "John Wesley, Music Critic," pages 82-84. While his opinions ranged over the whole of church and theater music with religious lyrics, the latter characterized by Handel's *Messiah*, Wesley's attempts to set standards for congregational song may appear arbitrary, inconsistent, and perhaps uninformed. These qualities, however, are consistent with his improvisatory managerial style whereby he guided the societies' witness and work. For example, in our discussion of *Sacred Harmony*, we have shown the flexibility of Wesley's response to the increasing presence of choirs and keyboard instruments.

*Congregations, Organs, and Choirs*

After Wesley's death Methodist musical authority was taken over by the conferences (see pages 101-03) who attempted to deal with a host of issues including preachers' objections to the abridgment of their sermons to make room for more choir music, while others claimed that choir music was an important way to attract worshippers. This controversy was the beginning of the congregation's century-long downgrading from the primary musical ensemble to secondary status under the choir and organ; the latter by Victorian times was hailed the resounding winner, only occasionally silenced by power outages or the choir's a cappella offerings.

In the US during the nineteenth-century transition from rural revivalism to urban revivalism, Methodist musicians and hymnal editors set aside distinctly USA musical styles and forms in favor of Euro-Anglo styles. At the same time the musical-matrix of Methodism moved from participatory-congregational to passive-choir modes as choral music was imported into the church from its recreational, educational, and artistic roots in the community. This development by the mid-to-late twentieth century in some churches resulted in a staff of professional musicians, the stockpiling of impressive inventories of music-making paraphernalia, significant budgets, and the recruiting and organizing of hordes of choir-folk for the presumed task of forming, enabling, and supporting the congregation and its song—an objective long since forsaken in favor of musical performance, entertainment, social, and educational attributes and the numbers game—the latter the fleas that come with the hungry puppy named "Church Growth."

The inclusion of choirs and their repertory and performance practice in United Methodist worship has seldom been informed by Wesleyan theology and its implicit and explicit ethical concerns. Instead, music is generally justified by considerations of taste. Its vicarious offerings and performance standards have more affinity to Anglo-catholic sacramental theology and worship forms than congregational-centered evangelical worship. A further complication of this preoccupation with music-making is that musicians have too often convened and cultivated choirs within a stern work ethic, sans grace for those who sing or play wrong notes. The consequence is a flawed expression of Wesleyan Christian perfection. Holy and perfect music, the short-term and elusive goal of the church musician, ironically has also been tolerated and more often fostered by clergy whose preaching and liturgical leadership have diminished in quality and effectiveness in inverse proportion to the musician's ability to recruit, manage, and maintain a continuing supply of singers to perform at the mercy seat of musical grace. The crucial consequence is that United Methodist's music of the heart, once a province of the congregation, is now mostly sung by the choir to the congregation.

Erik Routley articulated the problems of attempting to sustain the repertory and performance practice of congregational song while accommodating the escalating performance needs of the choral establishment:

> But two things tend to put a brake on the congregational acceptance of new material [hymns] and their intelligent use of it. One is the enormous success of the choral tradition in church, attributable mainly to the apostleship of John Finley Williamson who founded Westminster Choir College in 1926. Today so many churches have so many vigorous choral programs that there is normally room only for three hymns in a morning service: and of course there is often no other service in the day, so that a congregation sings about 150 hymns a year, sometimes only 100. The repertory diminishes almost as the square of the diminution of singing opportunities: if you sing few hymns you are the more impatient if any are unfamiliar. Congregational adventurousness in musical matters is declining sharply, even if their taste is very gradually rising (Routley 1982, 97).

Other impediments to vital congregational song include the congregation's increasing dependence on the organ and instruments, dead carpeted worship spaces, the absence of music and hymnody in theological education resulting in the pastor-in-charge as a functioning illiterate in these disciplines, the practiced distinction in worship between preached word and sung word, and the failure of schools of music to inform church musicians as to their pedagogical tasks including the selection, teaching, leading, and accompanying congregational song. An additional problem is that the music of twentieth-century mainline hymnals has mostly been informed by the repertory and performance practice of choral and organ literature and hymn singing in academic worship settings.

Attempts by hymnal committees to balance this perceived academic orientation has brought forth an increase of new and old gospel hymns, spirituals, and a wide assortment of choruses, accommodations that have for the most part raised the congregation's comfort level and increased the entertainment value of worship. In these places hymns are seldom "the folk-song of the church militant," as Erik Routley (Routley 1959, 3), called them, but more likely religious jingles—bits and pieces of songs and hymns strung together in subliterate choruses of key evangelical or scriptural words, trifling disposable and disingenuous fusions of minimal music with stale fragrances of vital religious rhetoric.

### *Reconstruction of Congregational Song: New Music of the Heart*

The reconstruction of congregational song will occur and is occurring where distinctive and teachable tunes in a variety of musical styles and performance practices are joined with a functional, usable, and teachable hymnic repertory, and expressed in God's gifts of vocal music and tonal memory as vibrant hymn singing—singing that is active, inclusive, positive, compelling, and replicable; singing to teach and remember doctrine; singing to enhance advocacy-oriented preaching. The musician-teacher and preacher-teacher are, as they were in the Wesleys' day, the enablers of this new music of the heart—simple, singable, moving, memorable, and teachable congregational song; music of the heart that convenes the community, reminds it who and whose it is, prepares it for hearing, seeing, and responding to the proclaimed word and celebrated sacrament, and sends it forth for work and witness.

Many recent hymns, some from the so-called "hymnic explosion" of English language hymns that began in the in mid-1960's, are in the lineage of Wesleyan music of the heart. Those from Great Britain include

Fred Pratt Green's "Christ is the world's light" **(188)**, Fred Kaan's "Help us accept each other" **(560)**, and Sydney Carter's "Lord of the dance" **(261)**. Contributions from the US include Jaroslav J. Vajda's and Carl Schalk's "God of the sparrow, God of the whale" **(122)**, Carl Daw's "Like the murmur of the dove's song," set to Peter Cutts's exquisite BRIDEGROOM **(544)**, Brian Wren's impressive "This is a day of new beginnings," and "Bring many names," with Broadway-style tunes by Carlton R. Young: BEGINNINGS **(383)** and WESTCHASE.

From the impressive global and ecumenical Spanish language repertory is the late Cesáreo Gabaraín's "Tú has venido a la orilla" (Lord, you have come to the Lakeshore) **(344)**. Other contributions are Native-American hymns such as the Muscogee-Creek "Heleluyan" **(78)**; Asian-American hymns, including Boris and Clare Anderson's "God created heaven and earth" expressively set to a traditional Taiwanese melody by I-to-Loh **(151)**; and from the vast repertory of African-American song the bright Easter spiritual "He rose" **(316)**, and Charles A. Tindley's soulful urban gospel hymn "Beams of heaven as I go" **(524)**.

I conclude with seven recent examples of music of the heart: "Yesu— Gift of God to Humankind," a call-and-response Malawian credal hymn, translated and arranged by the celebrated missionary-poet Tom Colvin; a Christmas hymn, "Star—Child," by the talented New Zealand poet Shirley Erena Murray; Brian Wren's trinitarian hymn "Joyful is the dark," uniquely exploring the creative reaches of darkness; Lex Rivers' prayer "Lead me in the Way," composed for the congregation of St. John's on the Lake United Methodist Church, Miami Beach, where he is pastor; a characteristically inclusive Wesleyan communion hymn by the New Zealand musician-poet Colin Gibson; Swedish pastor-composer Per Harling's poignant "For sake of life" (För livets skull); and the simple and expressive Argentine folk hymn "Santo, santo, santo" (Holy, holy, holy).

# Yesu—Gift of God to Humankind

Words by Tom Colvin to a traditional
work song tune of Southern Africa

Sung to a strong drum beat

Hold as leader
continues

Leader    All

Leader:        All:

1. Yesu     Gift of God to humankind,
            came to set all people free.

2. Human    Yesu, perfect child of God,
            is like us in all but sin.

3. Godly    Grace of God in Yesu see,
            rich in God's humanity.

4. Sharing  Yesu shares our hopes and joys,
            all our pain and poverty.

5. Loving   In Yesu there's love for all
            love of God and neighbor too.

6. Helper   Yesu gives the burdened rest;
            anxious ones security.

7. Teacher  Yesu helps us all to learn
            Wisdom's own simplicity.

8. Brother  Yesu's loving grace and power
            bind us in one family.

9. Savior   Comes to save and not condemn
            lifts us up and sets us free.

10. Our God  Now we give ourselves again
             keep us yours eternally.

11. Yesu    Ale-  ale-  lu-  uya,
            Ale-  ale-  lu-  uya.

# Star—Child

Shirley Erena Murray, 1993

Carlton R. Young, 1994

1 Star——Child earth—Child, go - be - tween of God,
2 Street child, beat child, no place left to go,
3 Grown child, old child, mem'ry full of years,
4 Spared child, spoiled child, hav - ing, want - ing more,
5 Hope——for——peace Child, God's stu - pend - ous sign,

1 love Child Christ - Child heav - en's light - ning rod:
2 hurt child, used child no one wants to know:
3 sad child, lost child, sto - ry told in tears:
4 wise child, faith child know - ing joy in store:
5 down—to——earth Child, Star of stars that shine:

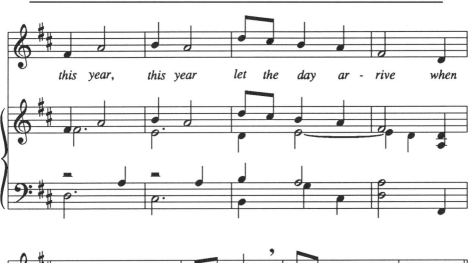

this year, this year let the day ar - rive when

Christ - mas comes for ev - ery one ev - ery-one a - live.

# Joyful is the dark

LINDNER

Brian Wren

Carlton R. Young

1 Joy - ful is the dark, ho - ly, hid - den
2 Joy - ful is the dark, Spir - it of the
3 Joy - ful is the dark, shad - owed sta - ble
4 Joy - ful is the dark cool - ness of the
5 Joy - ful is the dark depth of love di -

1 God, roll - ing cloud of night be - yond all
2 deep, wing - ing wild - ly o'er the world's cre -
3 floor; an - gels flick - er, God on earth con -
4 tomb, wait - ing for the won - der of the
5 vine, roar - ing, loom - ing thun - der - cloud of

1 nam - ing: maj - es - ty in dark - ness,
2 a - tion, silk - en sheen of mid - night,
3 fess - ing, as with ex - ul - ta - tion,
4 morn - ing; nev - er was that mid - night
5 glo - ry, ho - ly, haunt - ing beau - ty,

1 en - er - gy of love, Word - in - flesh, the
2 plum - age black and bright, swoop - ing with the
3 Ma - ry, giv - ing birth, hails the in - fant
4 touched by dread and gloom: dark - ness was the
5 liv - ing, lov - ing God. Hal - le - lu - jah!

1-4          5

1 mys - ter - y pro - claim - ing.
2 beau - ty of a ra - ven.
3 cry of need and bless - ing.
4 cra - dle of the dawn - ing.
5 Sing and tell the          stor - y.

1-4          5

# Lead me in the Way

Words and music by Lex Rivers

Arr: Carlton R. Young

*2nd time substitute: us, we, these, hearts.

go,_____ and teach this *wound-ed heart*_____

you should have me *go,_____ and teach this *wound-ed

that I* may know_____ the One who lives_____ is the

heart*_____ that I* may know the One who lives_____ is the

206

# This table is the Lord's

*for David Bromell and the Glenaven Methodist Church*

Words and music by Colin Gibson

GOTHENBURG

1 This ta - ble is the Lord's, and
2 Christ will not turn a - way who -
3 In sim - ple need we come, in
4 A joy, a grat - i - tude, a
5 Gath - er the world, dear Lord, as

1 all are wel - come here; the feast is laid, the
2 ev - er seeks His grace; be such the all - in -
3 sim - ple faith draw near; each brings a trou - bled
4 com - fort on the way; con - cerns un - known to
5 we are gath - ered here; that none be lost, none

1 wine, the bread, God's boun - ty all may share.
2 clu - sive love, that fills this ho - ly place.
3 se - cret world, a haunt - ing grief, a fear.
4 all but You and those for whom we pray.
5 stand a - lone, love's feast for all to share.

# For sake of life

Words and Music, Per Harling

Arr: Carlton R. Young, 1994

1 For sake of life the face of truth will
2 life the fields are be - ing
3 life a right - eous wrath needs
4 life our God be - came an

1 bright - en. For sake of life the seeds of hope will
2 seed - ed. For sake of life there's still growth in the
3 pow - er. For sake of life let streams of just - ice
4 in - fant. For sake of life he lived and died for

1 root._____ For sake of life the way of peace will
2 earth._____ For sake of life we'll share with all that
3 roll._____ For sake of life the springs of joy will
4 all._____ For sake of life the time of God is

1 light - en_____ for those who dare to walk_____ for sake of
2 need it_____ the bread from com - mon soil_____ for sake of
3 moth - er_____ the new - born child of hope_____ for sake of
4 con - stant._____ The king - dom is at hand_____ for sake of

life. 2 For sake of
life. 3 For sake of
life. 4 For sake of life._____

# Santo, santo, santo
## Holy, holy, holy

Argentine Folk Song

Arr: Carlton R. Young, 1994

San - to, san - to, san to. ¡Mi
Ho - ly, ho - ly, ho - ly. My

co - ra - zón te a - do - ra! Mi
heart, my heart a - dores you! My

co - ra - zón te sa - be - de - cir:
heart knows how to say to— you:

¡San - to e - res Se - ñor!
Ho - - ly are you Lord!

# References

Adams, Nelson F. 1973. "The Musical Sources for John Wesley's Tunebooks: the Genealogy of 148 Tunes." Ann Arbor: University Microfilms International.

Baker, Frank. 1962. *Representative Verse of Charles Wesley.* New York and Nashville: Abingdon Press.
_____. 1970. *John Wesley and the Church of England.* New York and Nashville: Abingdon Press.
_____. 1988. *Charles Wesley's Verse, An Introduction.* 2d ed. London: Epworth Press.
Baker, Frank, and George Walton Williams, eds. 1964. *John Wesley's First Hymn Book.* A Facsimile of *A Collection of Psalms and Hymns* with Additional Material. Charleston: Dalcho Historical Society.
Battishill, Jonathan. ca. 1770. *Twelve Hymns*, The Words by the Revd. Mr. Charles Wesley M.A. Late Student of Christ Church, Oxford. Set to Music by Mr. Jonathan Battishill. London: C. and S. Thompson in St. Paul's Church Yard.
Beckerlegge, Oliver A., and S T Kimbrough, Jr. 1990. *The Unpublished Poetry of Charles Wesley.* 3 vols. Nashville: Kingswood Books.
Benson, Louis F. 1915. *The English Hymn: Its Development and Use in Worship.* Reprint. Richmond: John Knox Press, 1962.
Berger, Teresa. 1994. *Theology in Hymns?* A Study of the Relationship between Doxology and Theology According to the *Collection of Hymns for the use of the People called Methodists* (1780). Trans. Timothy E. Kimbrough. Nashville: Kingswood Press.
Bett, Henry. 1937. *The Spirit of Methodism.* London: Epworth Press.
Blume, Friedrich. 1974. *Protestant Chuch Music.* New York: Norton.
Brown, Robert W. 1993. *Charles Wesley, Hymnwriter.* Bristol, England: Robert W. Brown, 42 Westover Road, Bristol BS9 3LT.
Brueggemann, Walter. 1988. *Israel's Praise.* Minneapolis: Augsburg.

Campbell, Ted A. 1991. *The Religion of the Heart. A Study of European Religious Life in the Seventeenth and Eighteenth Centuries.* Columbia: Univ. of South Carolina Press.

Clapper, Gregory S. 1989. *John Wesley on Religious Affections: his views on experience and emotion and their role in the Christian life and theology*. Metuchen, NJ, and London: Scarecrow Press.

Curnock, Nehemiah. 1909. *The Journal of the Rev. John Wesley, A.M.* 8 vols. Reprinted and enlarged. London: Epworth Press, 1938.

Dallimore, Arnold A. 1988. *A Heart Set Free*. Westchester, IL: Crossway Books.

Davies, Rupert E. 1976. *Methodism*. London: Epworth Press.

Doughty, W. L. 1958. "Charles Wesley, Preacher." *London Quarterly and Holborn Review*, 263-67. London: Epworth Press.

Douglas, Winfred. 1949. *Church Music in History and Practice: Studies in the Praise of God.* New York: Charles Scribner's Sons.

*The Dragon of Wantley.* 1817. Libretto by H. Carey. Music by John Frederick Lampe. New York: D. Longworth.

*Early Liturgies and Other Documents. 1872. Ante-Nicene Christian Library.* Alexander Roberts and James Donaldson eds. Vol. 24. Edinburgh: T. & T. Clark.

Ellinwood, Leonard. 1953. *The History of American Church Music.* New York: Morehouse-Gorham.

England, Martha Winburn. 1964. "The First Wesley Hymn Book." *Bulletin of the New York Public Library* 68 (4): 225-38.

Frost, Maurice. 1944. "John Wesley's Hymn Tunes." *Bulletin: Hymn Society of Great Britain and Ireland* 1: 5-7.

_____. 1952. "Harmonia Sacra, by Thomas Butts—I and II." *Bulletin: Hymn Society of Great Britain and Ireland* 3: 66-79.

_____. 1957-58. "The Tunes Associated with Hymn singing in the Lifetime of the Wesleys." *Bulletin: Hymn Society of Great Britain and Ireland* 4: 118-26.

Gealy, Fred D., Austin C. Lovelace, and Carlton R. Young. 1970. *Companion to the Hymnal* [1966]. Nashville: Abingdon Press.

Gill, Frederick C. 1964. *Charles Wesley: The First Methodist.* Nashville: Abingdon Press.

Glover, Raymond R. 1990. *The Hymnal 1992 Companion.* New York: Church Pension Fund.

Green, Richard. 1896. *The Works of John and Charles Wesley. A Bibliography.* London: Methodist Conference Office.

Gregory, W. L. 1958. "Charles Wesley's Hymns and Poems." *London Quarterly and Holborn Review*, 253-62. London: Epworth Press.

Halter, Carl, and Carl Schalk, eds. 1978. *Handbook of Church Music.* St. Louis: Concordia Publishing House.

Heitzenrater, Richard P. "Things seen and not seen—the World of Wesley's Diary." Unpublished lecture July 27, 1993. Cambridge, England: World Methodist Historical Society/Wesley Historical Society Conference.

*Hymns and Psalms. A Methodist and Ecumenical Hymn Book.* 1983. London: Methodist Publishing House.

*In Tune with Heaven: The Report of the Archbishops' Commission on Church Music.* 1992. London: Hodder and Stoughton.

Jones, Ivor H. 1990. *Music—A Joy For Ever.* London: Epworth Press.

Julian, John, ed. 1907. *A Dictionary of Hymnody.* 2 vols. Reprint. New York: Dover Publications, 1957.

Kimbrough, S T, Jr., ed. 1992. *Charles Wesley: Poet and Theologian.* Nashville: Kingswood Books.

_____. 1994. "Lyrical Theology." *Journal of Theology* 98:18-43. Dayton, OH: United Theological Seminary,

_____. 1993. *A Song for the Poor.* New York: General Board of Global Ministries of the United Methodist Church.

_____. 1993. Unpublished commentaries on Wesley hymns in correspondence with Carlton R. Young.

Lampe, John F. 1737. *A Plain and Compendious Method of Teaching Thorough Bass.* London: J. Wilcox. Facsimile ed. New York: Broude Bros., 1969.

_____ 1746. *Hymns on the Greater Festivals and Other Occasions.* Photocopied from the first edition in the library of Frank Baker.

Leaver, Robin. 1991. *'Ghoostly Psalmes and Spirituall Songes': English and Dutch Metrical Psalms from Coverdale to Utenhove, 1535-1566.* London: Oxford Univ. Press.

_____1994. "Lampe's Tunes," unpublished paper.

Leaver, Robin A., and James A. Litton, eds. 1985. *Duty and Delight, Routley Remembered.* Carol Stream, IL: Hope Publishing.

Lightwood, James T. 1898. "Notes on the Foundery Tune-Book." *Proceedings of the Wesley Historical Society* 1:116-17. London: Methodist Conference Office.

_____. 1900. "Notes on the Foundery Tune-Book." 2d Part. *Proceedings of the Wesley Historical Society* 6:147-17. London: Methodist Conference Office.

_____. 1905. "Tune Books of the Eighteenth Century." *Proceedings of the Wesley Historical Society* 4:101-08. London: Methodist Conference Office.

_____. 1905. *Hymn-Tunes and Their Story.* London: Charles H. Kelly.

_____. 1927. *Methodist Music in the Eighteenth Century.* London: Epworth Press.

_____. 1928. *Stories of Methodist Music: Nineteenth Century.* London: Epworth Press.

_____. 1955. *The Music of the Methodist Hymn-Book* [1933]. London: Epworth Press.

McCutchan, Robert Guy. 1942. *Our Hymnody: A Manual of the Methodist Hymnal* [1935]. 2d ed. Nashville: Abingdon-Cokesbury Press.

Martin, Dennis R. 1985. *The Operas and Operatic Style of John Frederick Lampe.* Detroit Monographs in Musicology No. 8. Detroit: Information Coordinators.

*The Methodist Hymn Book.* 1933. London: Methodist Conference Office.

Metzger, Bruce M., and Roland E. Murphy, eds. 1991. *The New Oxford Annotated Bible* [New Revised Standard Version]. New York: Oxford Univ. Press.

*Minutes of the Methodist Conference* [1744-1824]. 1862-64. 5 vols. London: John Mason. The "Large" *Minutes* are in 1: 443-675.

Moore, Mary Elizabeth Mullino. 1991. *Teaching from the Heart: Theology and Educational Method.* Minneapolis: Fortress Press.

Nason, Elias, and J. Frank Beale, Jr. 1895. *Lives and Labors of Eminent Divines.* Philadelphia: John E. Potter.

*The New Grove Dictionary of Music and Musicians*. 1980. Edited by Stanley Sadie. 20 vols. London: Macmillan.

Nuelsen, John L. 1972. *John Wesley und das duetsche Kirchenlied [John Wesley and the German Hymn]*. Trans. Theo Parry, Sydney H. Moore, and Arthur Holbrook. Keighley, England: Mantissa Press.

*Oxford Companion to Music*. 1970. Edited by Percy A. Scholes and John Owen Ward. London: Oxford Univ. Press.

*Oxford Dictionary of Quotations*. 1992. Edited by Angela Partington. 4th ed. London: Oxford Univ. Press.

Probert, J.C.C. 1978. *The Worship and Devotion of Cornish Methodism*. [No publisher indicated]

Reynolds, William J., and Milburn Price. 1987. *A Survey of Christian Hymnody*. Carol Stream, IL: Hope Publishing.

Routley, Erik. 1957. *The Music of Christian Hymnody*. London: Independent Press.

_____. 1959. *Hymns and Human Life*. 2d. ed. Grand Rapids: Eerdmans.

_____. 1967. *The Church and Music*: London: Duckworth.

_____. 1968. *The Musical Wesleys*. New York: Oxford Univ. Press.

_____. 1976. *Church Music and the Christian Faith*. Carol Stream, IL: Hope Publishing.

_____. 1979. *An English-Speaking Hymnal Guide*. Collegeville: Liturgical Press.

_____. 1981. *The Music of Christian Hymns*. Chicago: GIA Publications.

_____. 1982. *Christian Hymns Observed: When in Our Music God Is Glorified*. Princeton: Prestige Publications.

Saliers, Don E. 1991. *The Soul in Paraphrase*. 2d ed. Cleveland: OSL Publications.

Schilling, S. Paul. 1983. *The Faith We Sing*. Philadelphia: Westminster Press.

Schmidt, Martin. 1962, 1966. Trans. Norman Goldhawk. *John Wesley, A Theological Biography*. 2 vols. Nashville: Abingdon Press.

Seashore, Carl E. 1938. *Psychology of Music*. New York: McGraw-Hill.

Smith, George. 1866. *History of Wesleyan Methodism*. 3 vols. London: Longman, Green, and Roberts.

Stephens, John. 1827. *An address to the Methodists of Leeds, on the disturbed state of their Societies; delivered at the Old Chapel, on Sunday the 9th of December, 1817*. Leeds: Henry Cullingworth.

Stevenson, Robert M. 1953. *Patterns of Protestant Church Music*. Durham: Duke Univ. Press.

Temperley, Nicholas. 1979. *The Music of the English Parish Church*. 2 vols. Cambridge: Cambridge Univ. Press.

————. 1993. "The Lock Hospital Chapel." *Journal of the Royal Musical Association* 118: 44-72.

Thomas, Isaiah, and Marcus S. McCorison, eds. 1970. *The History of Printing in America*. 2d ed. Barre, MA: Imprint Society.

*The United Methodist Hymnal*. 1989. Edited by Carlton R. Young. Nashville: United Methodist Publishing House.

Wainwright, Arthur W., ed. 1993. *Wesley/Langshaw Correspondence*. Atlanta: Scholars Press.

Wainwright, Geoffrey. 1980. *Doxology. The Praise of God in Worship, Doctrine and Life*. New York: Oxford University Press.

Ward, John Owen, ed. 1970. *The Oxford Companion to Music*. London: Oxford Univ. Press.

Watson, Richard, and Kenneth Trickett, eds. 1988. *Companion to Hymns and Psalms* [1983]. Peterborough, England: Methodist Publishing House.

Werner, Eric. 1959. *The Sacred Bridge. The Interdependence of Liturgy and Music in Synagogue and Church During the First Millenium*. New York: Columbia Univ. Press.

Wesley, Charles [Jr.]. *Sacred Harmony*. A Set of Tunes Collected by the Late Rev. John Wesley. M. A. for the Use of Congregations in his Connexion. An Edition carefully revised and corrected by his Nephew, Charles Wesley Esq. London: T. Blanshard, 1822.

Wesley, Charles. 1849. *Journal of the Rev. Charles Wesley, M.A.* An Introduction and Occasional Notes, by Thomas Jackson. 2 vols. Reprint. Grand Rapids, MI: Baker Book House, 1980.

_____. 1994. *Catalog of the Charles Wesley Papers.* vol.1. Manchester: Methodist Archives and Research Center.

Wesley, John, ed. 1742. *A Collection of Tunes Set to Music, As they are commonly Sung at the Foundery.* London: A. Pearson. Reprint 1981. Bristol, England: Bryan F. Spinney.

_____. 1761, 1770. *Select Hymn With Tunes Annext.* Bristol: William Pine.

_____. 1872. *The Works of John Wesley.* 14 vols. London: Wesleyan Conference. Reprint, 1938. Zondervan Publishing House.

_____. 1931. *The Letters of the Rev. John Wesley.* Edited by John Telford. Standard ed. 8 vols. London: Epworth Press.

_____. 1980-91. *The Works of John Wesley.* Editor-in-Chief Frank Baker. Vol. 25: *Letters* I: 1721-39, edited by Frank Baker. Oxford: Clarendon Press, 1980; Vols. 1-4: *Sermons:* "An Introduction," edited by Albert C. Outler with a foreword by Richard P. Heitzenrater. Nashville: Abingdon Press, 1984-1991; Vol. 9: *The Methodist Societies.* Nashville: Abingdon Press, 1989; Vol. 11: *The Appeals to Men of Reason and Religion.* Nashville: Abingdon Press, 1975; Vol. 7: *A Collection of Hymns for the Use of the People called Methodists,* edited by Franz Hildebrandt and Oliver A. Beckerlegge. New York: Oxford Univ. Press, 1983; *Journals and Diaries* I: 1735-38, edited by W. Reginald Ward and Richard P. Heitzenrater. Nashville: Abingdon Press, 1988.

Wesley, Samuel. 1828. *Original Hymn Tunes, Adapted to Every Metre In The Collection by The Rev. John Wesley, A. M. Late Fellow of Lincoln College, Oxford, Newly composed and arranged for Four Voices, with a Separate Accompaniment for the Organ or Piano Forte, by Samuel Wesley.* London: Mayhew & Co.

White, James F. 1989. *Protestant Worship: Traditions in Transition.* Louisville: Westminster/John Knox Press.

Young, Carlton R. 1993. *Companion to the United Methodist Hymnal.* [1989] Nashville: Abingdon Press.

# General Index

(Major comments are noted by bold face numbers.)

*Graces Before Meat* (ca. 1746), 109
Green, Fred Pratt, 198
Green, Richard, 37
Gregory, John, 86, 90
Gregory, T. S., 29
"The Grounds of Vocal Music" (J. Wesley), 75-79

Halter, Carl, 21
Handel, George Frederick, x, 55, 71, 89, 90, 104, 105, 106, 116, 171, 178, 182, 194; tributes to by C. Wesley, 182; tunes composed for C. Wesley's texts, 182
Harling, Per, 198, **208-09**
*Harmonia Sacra* (Butts, ca. 1756), xi,55, 66, **68-70**,79, 105, 110, 170
"heart," in J. Wesley's sermons, 12-18; use of in expressing religious affectations, 10-11; use of in scripture, 9-10; in Wesleyan revival, 12-18, 191-92, 197
Heermann, Johann, 22
Heitzenrater, Richard P., 34
Herbert, George, ix, 25, 38
Hildebrandt, Franz, xii
Hill, Rowland, 104
Hoare, Brian, xi
Holy Club; *see* Oxford Holy Club
Hopkey, Sophy, 36, 43, 44
Hopkins, John, 23
Hus, Jon, 20
hymn singing, in English worship, 24-26, 193; role of in Christian worship, 19-20; recent developments in, 197-98; impediments to, 195-97; in Lutheran worship, 21; as lyrical theology, 29-30; in early Methodist worship practice, **56ff;** as metrical psalmody, 22; influence of Moravians on, 56, 58-59; psalm singing as, 56-57; influence of Vaughan

Williams on, 194; J. Wesley's "Directions" for, 72-73
Hymn Society in the United States and Canada, xvii
Hymn Society of Great Britain and Ireland, xv
*Hymns Ancient and Modern* (1861), 193
*Hymns and Psalms* (1983), xi
*Hymns and Sacred Poems* (1739, 1740, 1742, 1749), 54, 160, 165, 169, 170, 171, 193
*Hymns for those that seek and those that have Redemption in the Blood of Jesus Christ* (1747), 107, 178
*Hymns of Intercession for All Mankind* (1758), 168
*Hymns on the Great Festivals and Other Occasions* (Lampe, 1746), xvi, 31, 66, 68, 69, 104, 105, **108-10**

Ingalls, Jeremiah, 170
Ingham, Banjamin, 34

Jones, Ivor H., 20, 30
*Journal* (C. Wesley), 118-22; conversion references in, 123, 155; congregational singing references in, 120; entries, **122-52**, 185; references to the sacrament in, 121, 125, 133
*Journal* and *Diaries* (J. Wesley), 46; entries, 42-45, 178
Julian, John, 37

Kaan, Fred, 198
Kelway, Joseph, 174, 176
Ken, Thomas, 25, 49
Kimbrough, S T, Jr., x, xii-xiv, 6, 28, 73-74, 166, 176, 185
Knibb, Thomas, 67

# Index of Titles and First Lines of Poems

(Titles are noted in italic)